DEDICATION

I would like to dedicate this book to Agent Black Rose.

Agent Black Rose survived when 50 million others did not.

A survivor.

www.AustrianRose.com

GOD, GOLD, GUNS, GEAR, GRUB and GET out of town!

By: Captain Tony Taylor

ISBN: 978-1-300-64385-2

www.captaintonytaylor.com
630-209-8461

CaptainTonyTaylor@gmail.com

TABLE OF CONTENTS

INTRODUCTION

SURVIVAL

What does it mean to "survive"? "I am just trying to survive." My father, an octogenarian, always SAYS (presence tense), "I'm just trying to survive."

My highly decorated father, an E-9, survived three army tanks being blown out from underneath him. My father survived Jim Crow, the Great Depression, Agent Orange and depleted uranium. My mother survived after seeing 50 million people die in World War 2. My grandfather was not from Germany but he was forced to work in Hitler's army. He survived, millions of others did not survive.

Survival.

I survive in Chicago the murder capitol of the world. How do you survive in a country that has a quarter million pages of laws? How do you survive in a country with red light cameras on every corner? How do you survive in a country that is number one in divorce and prisons? Taking some time to learn some prepping and survival techniques is time well spent. Only a fool would complain about not having to have used his spare tire.

I am Captain Tony Taylor, I am a survivor. I have a knowledge base from knives to nukes. In this manual, I share my half century of skills, ability, knowledge and experience. You can get to the top of your game if you survive your competition. My father, a survivor, taught me: poor, prior, planning, produces poor performance. A survivalist's game plan is: Well studied-Well planned-Well executed.

Survival is the objective of this manual. The objective is obviously not a nice flowing cunningly devised fable about preparedness written in dulcet tones. A survival manual scribbled on the back of C ration boxes with a cold muddy hand and dangling participles is no less efficacious.

My survivalist instructors were not philologists, they butchered the king's English, but they kept me from getting butchered. My hope is to impart to you some nuggets that can help you survive this fire fight called life. My speech was not with enticing words of man's wisdom like your silver tongue politicians.

I hope you survive...row well and live.

TEST QUESTIONS

1. Is preparedness just a matter of buying another gun or is it a total package?
2. Will the first one you run to for help be the top cause of death?
3. Why is a one dollar paper mask an absolute survivalists essential?
4. What is one of the best survival foods?
5. What is a talking lamp post?
6. What is Universal Precaution?
7. What is the number one deterrent to crime?
8. What is the weapon retention distance?
9. Should you buy a dog dish if you don't have a dog?
10. What is the average distance of a fire fight?
11. How many inches of water does it take to wash your car into a ditch?
12. What natural disaster causes the most damage every year?
13. What is normalcy bias?
14. How many days did it take New York to dumpster dive with Sandy?
15. How will most people die from a Nuke?
16. What are drones looking for?

17. Who do snipers shoot first?
18. What is democide?
19. What is B.O.B?
20. What is a Boy Scout Prepper?
21. How long will the average person survive in the wild?
22. At what temperature will you die?
23. How long did it take for people to kill for food?
24. How long did it take for people to kill people for food?
25. What is the difference between sheep, sheep dogs and wolves?
26. Does a switch blade drone hurt?
27. How do you break a hand lock?
28. What is the first question to ask hostage taker?
29. Should you kneel in a fire?
30. What is the one thing you must remember in war?
31. How much bacteria can dance on the head of a pen?
32. Who is the number one causality in war?
33. What is the lesson of Ann Frank?
34. Is a duck the best guard pet?
35. How far away can a bear smell you?
36. Why do snipers love cigarettes?
37. NOW do you know why you should buy this book now?

38. What is the frost line?
39. What is COG?
40. Can you out run Big Dog?
41. How do I know you have loved ones?
42. Should you walk over hills?
43. Would you be mad if you had a spare tire and did not use it?
44. What are the two biggest threats to your guns?
45. How many seconds should you run before cutting?
46. How far away can you be seen?
47. When does the earth curve?
48. How do you instantly increase night vision?
49. What is light disciple?
50. What is sound discipline?
51. How many soldiers die from Friendly Fire?
52. Do soldiers say, "Duck duck?"
53. How many uses are there for duck tape?
54. Should you wear a floppy hat?
55. How many people die from empty guns?
56. What are the ten preparations to draw down a country?
57. How long does it take to incapacitate your country?
58. Will your country last forever?
59. Can an emergency happen to you?
60. Should you travel before the grid goes down?

61. Do you want to be on the last train out?
62. How close to the edge do you want to be?
63. What is the Doctrine of Fleeing?
64. What Would Jesus Do-Was Jesus a prepper?
65. How much does a First Aid course cost?
66. What is an ORP?
67. Should you speak in the clear?
68. Do tracers work both ways?
69. How long does it take to learn sign language?
70. How valuable is a solar blanket?
71. Should you be concerned when people like me disappear?
72. What is the first thing you reach for when the grid goes down?
73. Can the grid go down?
74. How long does the average currency survive?
75. How many paper currencies fail?
76. What is layering?
77. What is bad weather?
78. What percent of your money is guaranteed by cash?
79. What is a statist?
80. At what food cost to income ratio do people start rioting?
81. Can you out run a tornado?

82. How would an EMP change my life?
83. How often does the Sun have solar flares?
84. How valuable is mobility when things get ugly?
85. What does it mean to shoot, move and communicate?
86. Should you over communicate?
87. What percent of successful people have written plans and goals?
88. What is the difference between an goal and a dream?
89. What is a CCMP?
90. What is MBO?
91. What is a mobilization exercise?
92. What percentage of money is cash?
93. How long does it take to devalue your currency?
94. What is poverty control?
95. What are Capitol controls?
96. How many battles did Che Guevara win?
97. How many officers were killed in the French and Indian War?
98. Have camps ever been used in history?
99. Would people in suits lie to you?
100. What is appeal to authority?
101. How many defensive positions survived?
102. What were the White Russians used for?

103. How many countries are used in national levels exercises?

104. Are the communist our friends now?

105. What percent of the kings died natural deaths?

106. What has to happen before you can have a mass slaughter?

107. What is the Georgia Guide Stones?

108. How did most of the people die under Stalin?

109. How many people died under Moe?

110. Is depleted uranium depleted?

111. What is the most poisonous thing in the world?

112. How can you tell if water is radioactive?

113. What is the most poisonous none radioactive thing on earth?

114. Are crazy people dangerous?

115. What is the preferred weapon of crazy people?

116. What is the highway of death?

117. What is a zombie?

118. What is a zombie apocalypse?

119. Should you tie up a bad guy in front or back?

120. What percent of people are natural born killers?

121. What ratio of people are predators?

122. What is the element of surprise?

123. Is lack of proper nutrition the cause for natural

death?

124. What is the magic bullet for an atomic blast?

125. What is Run Up?

126. What is the most toxic “food” in your grocery store?

127. What is the number one cause of death for children?

128. What is your best legal, light and effective weapon?

129. What is currency in every country except America?

130. Who moves faster soldiers or a woman and a baby?

131. When should you start to prepare for emergencies?

132. Ignorance is bliss, but is it safe?

133. Is it fear mongering to warn someone that their house is on fire?

134. What is the quick and the dead?

135. Is your unprepared neighbor your biggest threat?

136. How far will the hoards travel for food?

137. Is most intelligence counter intelligence?

138. How much pain medicine do soldiers use?

139. How long does it take for a cut to rot?

140. Who has a higher survival rate, a team or individual?
141. What was the top cause of death in the Civil War?
142. What percent of causalities are civilians?
143. What percent of people died in the Great Plague?
144. How many died from head shots?
145. How many Jews died in World War 2?
146. What is the Sound of Music?
147. How long did it take for people to kill people for food?
148. How many Nazi conquered Warsaw?
149. How long did the Warsaw Jews hold off an army?
150. What is red list?
151. What is blue list?
152. Are you on a list?
153. How many Germans died in World War 2?
154. When do they come for Red List?
155. What is the first thing they turn off?
156. When is it time to defend yourself?
157. Should wait to punch before or after you are

dazed?

158. What is siege?

159. Should you answer the door?

160. Is it better to be carried by six or tried by twelve?

161. What are your chances of getting cut in a knife fight?

162. Is long hair an advantage in fighting?

163. How many states declared emergencies?

164. Which hemisphere is more radioactive?

165. Why will lines kill you?

166. How do you pick cuffs?

167. What is triage?

168. How far should you stay from the road?

169. What animal should you eat after?

170. How much heat do polar bears give off?

171. What color is the best for a light filter?

172. What is your greatest financial threat?

173. When should a hostage try to escape?

174. Why are cigarettes a free head shot?

175. What weapon do you never put on safe?

176. How heavy should your pack be?

177. Does your night light convert into a flashlight?

178. Is most war physical or psy-op?

179. Do you have potassium iodide?

180. Should you drink the water?

181. When are you ready to live?

182. Who shoots a hostage first?

183. What are they spraying?

184. What is a false flag?

185. Why will slugs kill you?

186. Why do you need direct sun light?

187. What is Berry Berry?

188. What is benign denial?

189. What is cognitive dissonance?

190. Who wins, a wrestler or a boxer?

191. What is a internationally recognized currency in every country except America?

192. Will the first one you run to be the the number one cause of unnatural death?

193. Do you have potassium iodide in your medicine cabinet?

194. Do you have a Bug Out Bag in your car?

195. Why do you tie down the second antenna?

196. What two things do Medal of Honor winners have in common?

197. You have met old pilots. You have met bold pilots, but have you met any old bold pilots?

198. Do wolves attack the weak or the strong?
199. Are you a soft target?
200. Are most hacks technical or simple?
201. Are most high end heists inside jobs?
202. Who is a threat if you have assets?
203. What should you name a tea cup poodle?
204. Why will a holster save your life?
205. Will a gun go off when you are trying to disarm someone?
206. Are the Illuminati historical figures?
207. Can a 99 pound woman beat up a man?
208. Do criminals respect shot guns held by women?
209. Do you want a well organized, well written book or do you want to live?.
210. Would I appreciate any helpful advice?
211. How many real chin ups can the average woman do?
212. Would you bet on a professional boxer or grandma with a pistol?
213. Will the fire kill you or the smoke?
214. How many bullets are exchanged in the average fire fight?
215. What percent of the population are soldiers?
216. What is the average distance of a fire fight?

217. How long does the average fire fight last?

218. Can a pencil neck change a flat tire?

219. What was the Roman word for negotiate?

220. What is the Byzantine Peace model?

221. What does it take to incite a violent attacker?

222. What are your chances of losing your weapon?

223. Should you turn your back on a hostage taker?

224. What are your chances of shooting yourself in the foot?

225. What country is safe?

226. How many data banks have your information?

227. How many people have files on them?

228. What is Going Dark?

229. What percentage of people will go quietly in the night?

230. Why do you get away from the "Flag Pole"?

231. What is Off the Grid?

232. What percent of people have passports?

233. What is your probability of dying?

234. What are the top three causes of death?

235. What is one of the most dangerous things you can do in a day?

236. How many drinks do you drink before you are impaired?

237. Do you have a greater chance of winning the lottery or dying on the way to buy a ticket?

238. How many InfoWar terms do you need to be conversant in alternative media?

239. What is more dangerous, a knife or a fork?

240. How many major media outlets did J. Paul Morgan buy out?

241. Who said, Make it big and make it burn?

242. Who is Edward Bernays?

243. What is the first department that Bernays renamed?

244. Who said propaganda had to be simple?

245. Is the cover story fast or true?

246. How do you know a politician is lying?

247. What do it mean when they say they are taking you to a safe place?

248. Why do people believe TV?

TEST ANSWERS

Is preparedness just a matter of buying another gun or is it a total package?

It is amazing to me that people will here about a preparedness issue and there only answer is add another pistol to there huge pistol safe collection. A more comprehensive approach might be buy some potassium iodide, maybe a water filter. Spend some time and money on traveling and checking out some fall back positions. Preparedness is not buying another gun and sitting and watching a reality TV show about cow tipping.

Will the first one you run to for help be the top cause of death?

If someone waxes eloquent about preparedness and doesn't mention democide, they missed the boat. The number one cause of unnatural death is your country going rogue and killing you. If a person wants to debate about which rocket stove is the best and not address the 800 pound gorilla in the room then he is either and operative, a fool or both. 300 million murdered citizens agree with me.

Why is a one dollar paper mask an absolute survivalists essential?

A simple paper mask can protect you from many emergency scenario threats.

What is one of the best survival foods?

Peanuts, always have some un-shelled peanuts in your car and your bug out bag.

What is a talking lamp post?

If you live in Amerika you are under surveillance by hundreds of cameras every day. A prepper needs to be aware of the nature and capacities of the surveillance to which you are being subjected. There are certain emergency scenarios that you need to know who is watching and listening to you.

What is Universal Precaution?

Universal Precaution is the concept that you simply can not know who has what disease so you use universal precautions with everyone. This principle expands past medical issues.

What is the number one deterrent to crime?

Light.

What is the weapon retention distance?

21 feet, therefore should you let someone get with 21 feet of you?

Should you buy a dog dish if you don't have a dog?

Dog or dog gone have a shiny big dog dish on your front and back porch that says, “Killer”.

What is the average distance of a fire fight?

The length of a car.

How many inches of water does it take to wash your car into a ditch?

Sometimes less than six.

What natural disaster causes the most damage every year?

Floods

What is normalcy bias?

Your biggest battle is not physical, it is the battle for your mind and spirit. You have to fight the normalcy bias that says, “Hey everything is normal”. It's not normal, it's a bloody mess and until you get that, you and yours have no hope of developing a serious preparedness program.

How many days did it take New York to dumpster dive with Sandy?
Three

How will most people die from a Nuke?
Thyroid disorders, that's why you should be choking down potassium iodide in a nuclear situation "as directed." Thousands die from the melt down, millions die from the fall out on thyroids.

What are drones looking for?
According the Health Ranger Mike Adams, drones love light, heat and lines. That's why you need a floppy hat like Israel soldiers use. We are of course assuming you would like to keep your head attached to your body.

Who do snipers shoot first?
Commo gets shot first, then the fool with the fancy weapons yelling instructs to everyone else. The point man is safe. Vets know you want to look just like the next Joe, no shiny pearl handled pistols. How many opposition officers we killed in the French and Indian War? All of them except one the Indians said God would not let us kill. How many of Sergeant Slattery's officers were killed? All of them. Be not many masters. There is an advantage to staying under the radar, away from the flag pole. Spouting whales get harpooned. My rich Jewish business man millionaire friend always had a small but noticeable rip on the left sleeve elbow of ALL of his sweaters. They never realized that "pitiful" poor old man could buy their restaurant and sell it for scrap.

What is democide?
Democide is death by government. That is your number one threat. Get that point or you are just a Boy Scout Prepper who

is learning how to tie knots and start fires with Boy Scout juice. You are kidding yourself if you are having a conversation about preparedness and not addressing Democide.

<u>What is B.O.B?</u>
Bug Out Bag. It should be packed and ready to go. Buy a duplicate of what ever you think you need so you don't need to get into it and mess with. Have one in your car also.

<u>What is a Boy Scout Prepper?</u>
I used to be a Boy Scout. I have nothing against Boy Scouts, but if you think that just developing camping skills will save you you are terminally naive.

<u>How long will the average person survive in the wild?</u>
A few days.

<u>At what temperature will you die?</u>
Wikipedia says: "Heat is lost more quickly in water than on land. Water temperatures that would be quite reasonable as outdoor air temperatures can lead to hypothermia. A water temperature of 10 °C (50 °F) often leads to death in one hour. Water is 29 times more efficient at stripping your heat, therefore stay dry.

<u>How long did it take for people to kill for food?</u>
One week

<u>How long did it take for people to kill people for food?</u>
Two weeks. My father was a kid during the deadliest siege in history, Leningrad, 900 days, well over half a million dead. Within two weeks the city was turned into a Zombie Apocalypse. Cannibalism is real. Once you've seen it, all the petty debating about the efficacy of preparedness goes out the window. Many times in history siege victims been reduced to

selling all the have for pigeon dung. The pilgrims were reduced to eating peas measured out one at a time. I have Russian friends who were reduced to baking leaves and eating grass. I have friends who have tried to stave off starvation by literally eating mud pies. For powdered pudgy puny people that have never missed a meal, preparedness is boorish. For people that have gone a couple of weeks without food, preparedness is quite rational. Christians should be fasting. They should have some concept of hunger.

What is the difference between sheep, sheep dogs and wolves?
Most people are sheep. True predictors are tough but are only one in ten thousand. The only thing tougher than the wolf is the guy who goes and gets him and drags him in in a bag or chains.

Does a switch blade drone hurt?
You will not be prepared for Skynet if you don't understand how small and deadly drones can be. A shot gun round on a hand sized switch blade drone can remove you from the land of the living. Don't underestimate their lethality by their awkwardness or small size, that can be a fatal error.

How do you break a hand lock?
It's the basic blocking and tackling that wins and loses the game. If one in the group of rioters grabs your wrist with both of his hands and you pull straight back, you lose. Notice that he has eight fingers under your wrist and only two thumbs on the top of your wrist. I am assuming your arm is stronger than his thumb. Grab your captured hand with your free hand and pull up. Use your two arms to pull up against his two thumbs, now run.

What is the first question to ask hostage taker?
It entirely possible that you can find yourself hostage in a number of break down of civilization scenarios. All the

bravado in the movies you have watched are scripts written by pencil necks who have never had their noses bloodied. Try to talk down a altercation. Most of the the time you can. Don't say let's end this, he may oblige. Don't ask about his mother or family that might be a sore point. Start with a question with the least probability of back wash: “Do you want a cigarette?” The next question to deescalate is: “What kind of cigarettes do you like?” NOTE: I hate cigarette, but the clown who captured your loved one probably does. If all negotiations break down just get him to look out the window for the red dot on his forehead.

Should you kneel in a fire?

I have found that walking upright through a room full of super heated smoke tends to be hurtful. It is almost always better to take a knee and crawl to reduce your temperature exposure by hundreds of degrees. I lost a partner on a call because of a simple action. It's the little foxes that spoil the vine.

What is the one thing you must remember in war?

The one thing that you must remember in war is that you are at war. My father taught me that a lot of people died because they somehow forgot they were in a war zone. My father's singular focus was to make it back alive. He said he did not sleep for a year. I understand what that means. I woke up and went into the bathroom and found a tub full of mud from a war zone I knew my daddy had made it home alive. Ever after the war I never saw my dad wake up. He was always gone for work at 0 dark thirty. Most people are not vigilant. Most people have a Que Sera, Sera world view. We have been called to vigilance. Even our founding fathers said the price of freedom is eternal vigilance.

How much bacteria can dance on the head of a pen?

Most people in the Civil War died of disease. In the military you spend half your time fighting the bad guys and half your time fighting the elements. The Holy Scriptures took the time to instruct the soldier to cover their dung, even dogs have that much sense. People need to know that the little foxes spoil the vine. That doesn't make for dramatic TV shows but it is the truth. Be vigilant of germs. Sergeant Slattery almost ended his decorated octogenarian life early from germs. Napoleon the world conqueror was fallen by little green apples. For the lack of a nail a horse and a battle can be lost. Good coaches spend a whole day teaching their men how to tie their shoes properly. Five million bacteria on the head of a pen can mean the difference between survival and demise. Daily I see people eat with unwashen hands.

<u>Who is the number one causality in war?</u>
Children. Many people try to romanticize war. There is nothing romantic about a bunch of dead babies. Sergeant Slattery did not find it amusing to find a child with a bullet in her head. Single guys may not be very concerned about prepping. They figure they can just go sleep in the back of their pick-em-up truck. When you have precious little ones, prepping goes to a whole new level. Woe unto them that have kids in that day. With kids Prepping gets a lot hard and a lot more urgent.

<u>What is the lesson of Ann Frank?</u>
The Franks waited too long and lost it all. The Sound of Music got out early enough and are now living in Vermont.

<u>Is a duck the best guard pet?</u>
I don't know about ducks but the eccentric rich used geese to surround their mansions because they will alert on the drop of a dime.

<u>How far away can a bear smell you?</u>
A polar bear can smell a seal popping out of the water ten miles away. That is the problem about hunting bear is for the

first ten minutes you are hunting the bear then the bear is hunting you.

Why do snipers love cigarettes?
Sergeant Slattery said, The Brits learned a hard lesson in the Boer War, "Never light three on a match." After three puffs in the dark any sniper worth his salt could deliver a head shot.

NOW do you know why you should buy this book now?
==

What is the frost line?
Frost line is how deep the frost grows. Snowline is how high the snow stays. The cold line to pay attention to is, are you living in a geographical area where if the grid went down it would be difficult to survive.

What is COG?
The government is extremely concerned about Continuity Of Government. Meanwhile the media constantly hammers the message that you are crazy if you make preparations for any state of emergency. Tell the media to come save you when there is an emergency.

Can you out run Big Dog?
Four legged robots can hunt you through the woods. A two legged robot can out run any human. If you know nothing of these matter the you receive the official Boy Scout Prepper of the year award. You need to up your game.

How do I know you have loved ones?
I know you have loved ones if you have bought a water filter.

Should you walk over hills?
Never silhouette yourself coming over the top crest of a hill.

Would you be mad if you had a spare tire and did not use it?
Time spent prepping is not wasted time.

What are the two biggest threats to your guns?
Rust and politicians.

How many seconds should you run before cutting?
A normal shooter can not put a bead on you if you zig while he zags every three seconds.

How far away can you be seen?
The curve of the earth is 17 miles. What can be seen can be hit. What can be hit can be killed.

When does the earth curve?
The curve of the earth is 17 miles. For map reading point to point, set your direction on something on the horizon and keep moving.

How do you instantly increase night vision?
Look slightly over your target. You have too many color cones in the center of your eye for good night vision.

What is light disciple?
You must learn to use light discipline in a grid down situation. Everybody is not your friend. New York scared people with the lights on, imagine neighborhoods with no lights at night. Use your light without making yourself a target. Have verbal challenges.

What is sound discipline?
Old school dog tags, which I still wear, sound like a cow bell. You learn real quick to tie them puppies down and anything else that shakes rattles or rolls.

How many soldiers die from Friendly Fire?
Some estimates are as high as twenty percent. Only in the movies can you shot hundreds of rounds and the hero walks away unscathed.

Do soldiers say, "Duck duck?"
Soldiers do not say, "Duck, Duck"; they only say "Duck". You must learn in a "sterile cockpit" environment it's no clowning around, just the quick and the dead.

How many uses are there for duck tape?
Infinite, get some.

Should you wear a floppy hat?
Ask the Israel soldiers who are concerned about predictors, reapers and global hawks.

How many people die from empty guns?
Too many sad funerals for people not handling weapons well.

What are the ten preparations to draw down a country?
Watch Naomi Wolf's video on YouTube The End of America.

How long does it take to incapacitate your country?
If you think about it, key word being "think", it really doesn't take long to cripple any country. You might want to develop your preparedness program BEFORE someone shows you how fast your infrastructure can be turned into "kiddles" and bits.

Will your country last forever?
No. Daniel told us about five empires and yours is not one of them.

Can an emergency happen to you?

How is it that people sit back with a bowl of popcorn, watching the news thinking every state has a state of emergency except theirs?

<u>Should you travel before the grid goes down?</u>
Traveling to check out a Plan B is a delightful weekend getaway UNTIL the grid goes down. Once the grid goes down traveling will be a heralding epic journey, fraught with difficulties.

<u>Do you want to be on the last train out?</u>
I believe it was Survivalist Stewart who said, You better be on the train BEFORE the last train out.

<u>How close to the edge do you want to be?</u>
I you were debating about which driver to take you along the dangerous cliff trail. Would you hire the one who brags about how close to the edge he can get? Would you hire the one who doesn't want to get you near the edge of the cliff? I know old pilots and I know bold pilots. I just don't know any old bold pilots. When in doubt take the conservative route. Tragically, medal of honor winners have two things in common: one they are young and two they are dead.

<u>What is the Doctrine of Fleeing?</u>
What did Paul do when his enemies were gathering in the city to kill him? Paul did not form an army an attack his enemies. Paul was let down over the wall in a basket and he fled. Live at peace with all men as much as lieth in thee. Many people are not strangers to punching someone in the mouth, but survivors are the ones who try to avoid conflict. Hitler allowed the French to surrender and lost no troops. Even the Ram Alexander by passed the citadel to conquer the world.

What Would Jesus Do-Was Jesus a prepper?
Jesus said, He that hath no sword, let him sell his garment, and buy one.

How much does a First Aid course cost?
Far less than the cost of being uneducated and dying from a simple ailment.

What is an ORP?
You are a fool if you don't believe in Murphy's Law. If anything can go wrong it will go wrong at the worst possible time. The best planned and organized mission can go bust. You should always set up and Organizational Rallying Point FIRST, macro and micro. It never rains in the army just on the army.

Should you speak in the clear?
If you have had kids you have learned the painful lessons for the need of speaking in code.

Do tracers work both ways?
Yes.

How long does it take to learn sign language?
Sound disciple requires you learn basic macro sign language. Learning the hand alphabet could be a life savers for a survivalist.

How valuable is a solar blanket?
Priceless.

Should you be concerned when people like me disappear?
Yes. Jesus taught John. John taught Polycarp. Polycarp taught Chrysostom. Chrysostom taught the Syrian, the Syrian taught me, you can black bag me but nothing can separate me from

the love of God.

What is the first thing you reach for when the grid goes down?
First-Hand cranked light and candles. Second-something to stay warm. Third-A hand cranked radio to get some news hopefully without spin.

Can the grid go down?
The grid goes down all the time.

How long does the average currency survive?
27 years.

How many paper currencies fail?
All paper money in history collapses and goes to zero. Buy gold.

What is layering?
Layer your clothing.

What is bad weather?
European proverb, There is no such thing as bad weather just bad clothes.

What percent of your money is guaranteed by cash?
Learn what the phrase, "Fiat Currency" means.

What is a Statist?
Statist are sheeple who think the gabbment is a huge endless benevolent breast.

At what food cost to income ratio do people start rioting?
I believe Max Keiser sights 41 percent.

Can you out run a tornado?

Yes, in a well directed car.

How would an EMP change my life?
Everything you know will stop working instantly for the foreseeable future. You might want to have a Plan B.

How often does the Sun have solar flares?
24/7/365

How valuable is mobility when things get ugly?
Bunker mentality is only a temporary option.

What does it mean to shoot, move and communicate?
These are critical military survival elements.

Should you over communicate?
I tell the rookies, in life and death situations OVER communicate, don't worry about sentimentality.

What percent of successful people have written plans and goals?
7. My dad clawed his way through college one class at a time, with a household of eight. I used to go with him. Thank God I learned early that successful planning is reduced to writing.

What is the difference between a goal and a dream?
A goal has a deadline. Make a deadline for your preparedness plan or someone else will. Once it's up there is no end to tweaking.

What is a CCMP?
Clear Concise Mental Picture. Verbalizing your prepper plan to others helps identify fuzzy areas. Cloudy thoughts-wet words-crystallized pencils.

<u>What is MBO?</u>
Manage By Objective. Manage your prepper plan by objective then work backward.

<u>What is a mobilization exercise?</u>
The Threat forces would line up thousands of troops and tanks on the Fulga Gap supposedly for an exercise. We thought that it might be a good time for an exercise also. Run a mobilization exercise with your preparedness plan.

<u>What percentage of money is cash?</u>
3 percent paper cash.

<u>How long does it take to devalue your currency?</u>
3...seconds.

<u>What is poverty control?</u>
My mothers maiden name in Europe is Felder, which means field worker. Poverty has been used as a means of control for centuries. Hitler and Dracula kept their slaves just above starving. We keep you alive to serve this ship, row well and live. See the movie, Hunger Games neo-feudalism.

<u>What are Capitol controls?</u>
Hitler enacted capitol controls to keep the money from fleeing. Newsflash: Capital controls are being implemented in Amerika.

<u>How many battles did Che Guevara win?</u>
I don't want to answer that question because I will break your heart. My point is war and street fighting are messy and hard. All bets are off when the bullets fly and blood starts flowing. I have seen too many people go into shock and/or become a sobbing blubbering mess, neither of which is productive. The

fog of war and chaos theories come into effect in civilian or military emergencies. Incredible amounts of discipline, structure, and forethought are required to have a working preparedness plan when everything goes crazy. Things can instantly burst into a three ring circus keystone cop fire drill. Your preparedness plans and gear need to be solid.

How many officers were killed in the French and Indian War?
All of them were killed except the one the Indians said God would not let us kill. People rest on the leader to be a prepper. Your leader can be gone in a moment and you have a field promotion.

Have camps ever been used in history?
The British perfected camps against the white Africans in the Boer War. If camps were used against their own American orientals and American Indians, why do you think you can't go to a camp, “for your safety?”

Would people in suits lie to you?
When I speak to street wise audiences, I don't have to spend half the time convincing them that bad guys wear suits. Do not rich men oppress you, and draw you before the judgment seats? People would work harder on their prepper plans if they weren't brain washed into thinking that guys in suits are really loving slightly rotund purple dinosaurs.

What is appeal to authority?
Appeal to authority is one of the main psy-op control mechanisms, especially for older generation people. If people weren't brain locked they'd be fighting for air given the current circumstances.

How many defensive positions survived?
None.

What were the White Russians used for?

People think that our fine young men in uniform would never turn on us. Note Stalin used the White Russians to oppress the eastern Russians and used the eastern Russians to oppress the west white Russians. Sheeple can not bring themselves to believe that there are people in this world that would push a bullet in your head without batting an eye. Force your self to watch the YouTube videos of people begging before being shot in the head. It's a dark world and you need to have preparations for this present darkness. This world with devils filled.

How many countries are used in national levels exercises?

Over a dozen countries can be in your country for "friendly" war exercises. Another brilliant gabbament program.

Are the communist our friends now?

I have friends from all around the world. Yet, I am not naive enough to think that their countries leaders don't dream of a day when they can take everything you have. Dictators publicly talk about child-like gullible Amerikans and how the want to hang us with the rope we sell them. I have a plan B, do you?

What percent of the kings died natural deaths?

People that say they don't believe in conspiracies proclaim their own ignorance. History is filled from beginning to end with smoking back room deal making. Roosevelt said presidents are selected not elected. Too many of the kings died with a pillow over their face from an old friend. Many rulers have died from a "lone" gunmen who magically walks past scores of temporarily blind security staff. The world is unstable, you need to have prepper provisions for political upheaval.

What has to happen before you can have a mass slaughter?

You have to have mass disarmament.

<u>What is the Georgia Guide Stones?</u>
Satan's apples have to have warning labels. It wouldn't count if Satan chased Adam across the garden, tackled him and shoved an apple into his mouth. The Occult Aristocracy get a morbid thrill about telling you openly what they are going to do to you.

<u>How did most of the people die under Stalin?</u>
Stalin did not shot 20 million people in the head one at a time. Most war is psy-op. They have to get you to go along with your own destruction, preppers see the open information.

<u>How many people died under Moe?</u>
Moe didn't kill anybody but I am amazed at college educated kids I talk to who don't know Mao killed 80 million people. He crucified them and damned the rivers with their bodies.

<u>Is depleted uranium depleted?</u>
No. They used to tell the young wags to not sit on the ammo boxes. After they started peeing blood you would think they would connect the dots. You might want to take a few moments to familiarize yourself with Dr. Doug Rokke and The Dangers of Using Depleted Uranium. Just a thought. I'm just sayin', When your pee glows in the dark you may want to turn off the dancing bear video and watch some real news videos from Rokke and learn about D.U. Contamination.

<u>What is the most poisonous thing in the world?</u>
A word to the wise is sufficient, a million words to a fool is useless. A fool doesn't get it even though he is beaten by many stripes. The old men walked out of the factory when the platinum was brought in. The young bucks were lined up to take their jobs. Hey, do you want to clear out your family pictures out of your desk before you leave. No sonny you can

keep everything including the pencils. The most poisonous thing on planet earth is platinum. You can pluck your eye lash, rub it against platinum, put it in your old best friends breakfast eggs, he'll be dead before noon. Einstein said radiation is a terrible way to boil water. You are probably sitting within 50 miles of a nuclear plant. If the wind is blowing at 50 miles an hour, how many hours before your world slides off into a Hell zone. Preppers do their homework. Buy some potassium iodide and have a preparedness plan.

<u>How can you tell if water is radioactive?</u>
It is perfectly clear.

<u>What is the most poisonous none radioactive thing on earth?</u>
The mercury in the shots they will be giving you and your loved ones when they get you to walk in to the red dawn sports stadiums.

<u>Are crazy people dangerous?</u>
"Mentally challenged" people need no provocation, stay on your A game.

<u>What is the preferred weapon of crazy people?</u>
"Mentally challenged" people generally live in a knife culture. In a knife fight mentally brace yourself for the fact that you will get cut but probably not die. Focus, fight and do not go into shock.

<u>What is the highway of death?</u>
Most of our highways are parking lots under normal situations. When you have people panicking and running out of gas in front and behind, you may want a little forethought. Ask the poor civilian souls on the Baghdad highway of death.

<u>What is a zombie?</u>

Only God can raise the dead. You are paying to condition your kids to shot sick dirty “zombies”. I hope when the showers stop working these first person shooters don't mistake you for a sick dirty person knocking on their door for help.

What is a zombie apocalypse?
Ask the government they have official government web sites about it.

Should you tie up a bad guy in front or back?
In the back. What do you get for being a nice guy? You get a sharp stick in the eye. I would rather be tried by twelve than carried by six.

What percent of people are natural born killers?
1/7

What ratio of people are predators?
1/10,000

What is the element of surprise?
Go to the ant and consider her ways. See in nature who animals attack with a snap. Don't talk, sell woof tickets and lose the element of surprise. Learn the Art of War.

Is lack of proper nutrition the cause for natural death?
Dr. Joel Wallach is a great man. You should have him tell you why animals prefer muddy water. A prepper must understand nutrition and health.
www.tonytaylor.my90forlife.com

What is the magic bullet for an atomic blast?
Potassium iodide

What is Run Up?

You can't keep a big secret. You can't move a hundred thousand troops without someone knowing about it. Watch for a run up and get out of town, you never know when it will go hot. Jericho learned a hard lesson that 6 fake run ups is nothing compared to one going "dynamic".

<u>What is the most toxic "food" in your grocery store?</u>
Gum, even without the mind numbing aspartame, sweet poison. Preppers must have their game face on at all times. Being a brain numbed fluoride head won't serve you well when every synapse is needed.

<u>What is the number one cause of death for children?</u>
Diarrhea from dirty water, ergo buy a Life straw if you love your kids. Preppers agree, a house gravity feed water filter beats hugging toilet all night.

<u>What is your best legal, light and effective weapon?</u>
Pepper spray is prepper spray. Check your 250,000 pages of laws and ensure your masters will allow you to protect your family with pepper spray. Then go out immediately and buy some for anyone you like or love or are friends with.

<u>What is currency in every country except America?</u>
Gold. Mark Dice couldn't give away gold to Amerikans but the rest of the world understands.

<u>Who moves faster soldiers or a woman and a baby?</u>
My mom was a woman. I have nothing against women, but I can move a hundred soldiers faster than a woman and a baby. You may want to adjust your prepper plan accordingly.

<u>When should you start to prepare for emergencies?</u>
Now. My father taught me PPP-PPP Poor prior planning produces poor performance. If it has been done, it can be done.

Ignorance is bliss, but is it safe?
With much wisdom comes much sorrow, but sticking your head in the sand and your bum in the air is no protection from a charging lion.

Is it fear mongering to warn someone that their house is on fire?
No. Silly people say to preppers and preachers that we are fear mongering. These are the same people that don't die well. People talk like King Kong but when the heat is on they melt. If you sign up to witness an execution you might observe gangsta that go out kicking and crying.

What is the quick and the dead?
Speed, decisiveness and quick reaction are elements for survivors. Watch the classic black and white poignant scene where the "let them eat cake" queen frittered about for a hat and lost her head. Be decisive, get out of Dodge, seconds count.

Is your unprepared neighbor your biggest threat?
Joel Skoulsen makes it abundantly clear your unprepared neighbor is one of your biggest threats. The YouTube shows Mormon Beatles fanning out in a 360 degree fashion. There is an occasional popping sound when they over taking the slow ones for lunch.

How far will the hoards travel for food?
Five miles off the hard roads, you might want to camp past that.

Is most intelligence counter intelligence?
Yes. Never believe the cover story it's always out quickly, it's always simple and a lie. Preppers need to seek through the

Matrix. You need good Intel for good decision making. Technology has it's down side. Amerikans bragged they had a spy in the sky. Foreigners bragged they had a spy in the room. Get real intel but understand most is spin.

How much pain medicine do soldiers use?
Amerikans use six times as much pain medicine as foreigners. Amerikans worship the pill fairy. Preppers need to be healthy and strong in heart, mind and spirit Celente says.

How long does it take for a cut to rot?
Moments in a jungle.

Who has a higher survival rate, a team or individual?
Build a team and live, watch out for fakes, feds and mooches. Hudson learned, rice Christians run out when the rice runs out.

What was the top cause of death in the Civil War?
Disease.

What percent of causalities are civilians?
In World War I 10 percent, now with smarter bombs 90 percent.

What percent of people died in the Great Plague?
Half, eat your garlic and don't kill cats.

How many died from head shots?
In Vietnam most died from head shots. Boonie hats look cool in photo ops and berets are cute but neither stop bullets. Body armor may make you look fat, but holes in your chests create a sucking sound.

How many Jews died in World War 2?
Half, it gets personal when it's family.

What is the Sound of Music?
Sound of Music is the the movie shows your ticket out.

How long did it take for people to kill people for food?
Two weeks

How many Nazi conquered Warsaw?
I was told 12.

How long did the Warsaw Jews hold off an army?
28 days, that more then some countries, they should started before the decimation.

What is red list?
Vets, cops and guns owners. Other people that are considered threats are people who go church, believe in the constitution, question politicians and put their pants on one leg at a time.

What is blue list?
Non-vets, non-cops and non-gun owners. You can see pictures online of blue list people lined up a thousand deep with one solder watching them with six bullets in his gun. They are lined up to go to a safe place. Arbeit macht frei.

Are you on a list?
If you are breathing you are on a list.

How many Germans died in World War 2?
One third

When do they come for Red List?
3 AM

What is the first thing they turn off?

<u>When is it time to defend yourself?</u>
Before you are asked to walk out of the crowded restaurant into a dark lonely alley. Before you are told to get in a van with no windows or the trunk of a car. Before you are asked to dig your own grave in a lonely deserted muddy spot in the dark woods.

<u>Should wait to punch before or after you are dazed?</u>
Before.

<u>What is siege?</u>
Most exciting movies show the warriors valiantly charging the castle. The reality is you surround the city let them eat dung for a year and then clean up the skeletal remains. Expect to be impoverished before you are attacked.

<u>Should you answer the door?</u>
No

<u>Is it better to be carried by six or tried by twelve?</u>
12

<u>What are your chances of getting cut in a knife fight?</u>
High

<u>Is long hair an advantage in fighting?</u>
No

<u>How many states declared emergencies?</u>
All

<u>Which hemisphere is more radioactive?</u>
North by two times

Why will lines kill you?
Health Ranger Mike Adams says drones love lines and edges.

How do you pick cuffs?
An acquired skill.

What is triage?
IF you have to choose, let they guys with two legs blown off go and try to save the guy with one leg blown off.

How far should you stay from the road?
Five miles

What animal should you eat after?
The ones that have taste buds similar to yours.

How much heat do polar bears give off?
Zero. There are several lessons to learns from polar bears.

What color is the best for a light filter?
Red

What is your greatest financial threat?
Divorce

When should a hostage try to escape?
Initially

Why are cigarettes a free head shot?
Rudolph the Red nose rain deer effect.

What weapon do you never put on safe?
Pepper spray, your kids will only play with it once.

How heavy should your pack be?

1/3 your body weight

Does your night light convert into a flashlight?
It should, buy one a t Ace Hardware, smart product.

Is most war physical or psy-op?
Psy-op

Do you have potassium iodide?
Most of the deaths are from the fall out not the blast.

Should you drink the water?
No, filter it

When are you ready to live?
When you are ready to die.

Who shoots a hostage first?
The rescuers. When they come to save you, hit the ground and don't move.

What are they spraying?
Watch the video, “What are they spraying?”

What is a false flag?
The oldest trick in the book.

Why will slugs kill you?
Yes, they will drag you down. If a man shall not work, neither shall he eat.

Why do you need direct sun light?
Vitamin D is a super vitamin from the sun.

What is Berry Berry?

Too much of the same food in the wild.

What is benign denial?
Wishful thinking, deadly thinking.

What is cognitive dissonance?
A Jedi Mind trick you play on yourself to your own destruction.

Who wins, a wrestler or a boxer?
Wrestler, but boxer make better TV.

What is a internationally recognized currency in every country except America?
Gold. Smart pilot will have one tucked in his gear, the queen's face is recognizable around the world.

Will the first one you run to be the the number one cause of unnatural death?
Yes, democide.

Do you have potassium iodide in your medicine cabinet?
If you love life.

Do you have a Bug Out Bag in your car?
You should.

Why do you tie down the second antenna?
My father said, Be inconspicuous, if the bad guys only have one RPG it's going to the tank with the two antennas.

What two things do Medal of Honor winners have in common?
Sadly, dead and young.

You have met old pilots. You have met bold pilots, but have

you met any old bold pilots?
No

Do wolves attack the weak or the strong?
Weak, soft targets.

Are you a soft target?
No

Are most hacks technical or simple?
Simple.

Are most high end heists inside jobs?
Yes

Who is a threat if you have assets?
Everyone including dirty cops.

What should you name a tea cup poodle?
"Killer" engraved on your big shiny dog dishes on your front and back porch.

Why will a holster save your life?
A holster lock assures weapons retention in close environments.

Will a gun go off when you are trying to disarm someone?
Plan on it.

Are the Illuminati historical figures?
I lived there, their street is named after my mom. Understand your enemy. We are not ignorant of Satan's devices.

Can a 99 pound woman beat up a man?
Probably not, stop believing the TV. Adjust your game

accordingly.

Do criminals respect shot guns held by women?
Yes

Do you want a well organized, well written book or do you want to live?
I hope you support my feeble effort.

Would I appreciate any helpful advice?
Yes

How many real chin ups can the average woman do?
None. Don't have a defense strategy based on upper body strength you may be disappointed.

Would you bet on a professional boxer or grandma with a pistol?
I'm thinking granny. Guns are a great equalizer, that's why they want you disarmed.

Will the fire kill you or the smoke?
Smoke

How many bullets are exchanged in the average fire fight?
Domestically less than half a dozen, in a theater of war hundreds can be exchanged for one causality.

What percent of the population are soldiers?
About 7 percent. You may want to spend some face time with one for your preparedness planning. Very few people have a military prepper perspective.

What is the average distance of a fire fight?
About the distance of a car, domestically. Basic, quick shooting

skills is what you need. Most people won't use a Ghillie suit.

How long does the average fire fight last?
Domestically, a few seconds. Again, the quick and the dead. Bing, bang, boom, it's over "wit".

Can a pencil neck change a flat tire?
Probably not, but they may want to learn. If the grid goes down you may have to get your hands muddy.

What was the Roman word for negotiate?
There was none. When the Romans pulled a shore in Corinth, the powdered puff business men had made no provision for war. The Romans terms of negotiation were to chop all the males heads off. After Austria's coffers were drained they sent their ambassador past all the boy soldiers and told Napoleon, "France has need of life." Self crowned Napoleon said, "France has need of glory." Preppers need to understand the cruelty of leaders. The famed Tamil tigers fought for years then negotiated and were rewarded by being shot naked in a muddy field. Non-preppers don't sense the cost of failure. It costs to be a prepper. It cost a lot more not to be a prepper. See the pictures of the poor Jewish women on line getting shot as they crawl across the ground on their hands and knees. History is filled with millions of reasons to be a prepper.

What is the Byzantine Peace model?
All the enemies are dead. There will be no peace until the Prince of Peace comes.

What does it take to incite a violent attacker?
Nothing. Your civility does not ensure their civility.

What are your chances of losing your weapon?
Very high if you don't develop some skills, weapons retention

is critical.

<u>Should you turn your back on a hostage taker?</u>
No

<u>What are your chances of shooting yourself in the foot?</u>
Higher with a pistol than a shot gun.

<u>What country is safe?</u>
None

<u>How many data banks have your information?</u>
400

<u>How many people have files on them?</u>
All

<u>What is Going Dark?</u>
Dropping off the grid

<u>What percentage of people will go quietly in the night?</u>
Most

<u>Why do you get away from the “Flag Pole”?</u>
Stay away from the brass

<u>What is Off the Grid?</u>
Going dark

<u>What percent of people have passports?</u>
80

<u>What is your probability of dying?</u>
100 percent

What are the top three causes of death?
Heart disease, cancer and doctors not necessarily in that order.

What is one of the most dangerous things you can do in a day?
Get in a car.

How many drinks do you drink before you are impaired?
One. In a grid down scenario, you may want to stay 100 percent sober if you want to stay 100 alive.

Do you have a greater chance of winning the lottery or dying on the way to buy a ticket?
Dying

How many InfoWar terms do you need to be conversant in alternative media?
500

What is more dangerous, a knife or a fork?
Fork

How many major media outlets did J. Paul Morgan buy out?
All of them

Who said, Make it big and make it burn?
Hitler

Who is Edward Bernays?
The Austrian father of propaganda

What is the first department that Bernays renamed?
The department of war.

Who said propaganda had to be simple?

Hitlers people

Is the cover story fast or true?
Fast

How do you know a politician is lying?
Their lips are moving.

What do it mean when they say they are taking you to a safe place?
You are going to die.

Why do people believe TV?
I have no idea.

PART ONE-WHY BE A PREPPER

1. WHY PREP?

Who, what, when, where, how and why of being a prepper? WHY goes first because if you answer the WHY and the HOW will take care of its self. If people understood the urgency, the "WHY", then people would scramble to get the "HOW's.
Get the WHY and the HOW will take of its self.

The French have a saying, If you wish to converse with me you must define your terms. Why be a Prepper? What do you mean by Prepper? Someone who prepares for the eventuality that something might go wrong. This juxtapose to statist. Statist think the government is my daddy. Nothing can possibly go wrong ever. If anything did some how go wrong I can just lay on my back with my feet in the air and the gabbament will save me.

If you only understood how late it is, you would devour this book and run for another. Wise men still seek Him. If you are asleep at the wheel, dwelling in cities without walls then the best prepper book in the world can not save you.

Be careful HOW you hear. He that hath ears to hear, let him hear-Wer Ohren hat zu horen, der hore-El que tiene oildos para oir, olga

I'm a prepper, you're a prepper, wish we could all be a prepper, it would be safer for all of us.

I have family and friends that have a lot more resources than I do, but they have laughed at the idea of ANY preparedness. Just like Lots relatives laughed when he said leave Sodom and Gomorrah before it was destroyed. Many people have no sense of the clear reality starring down their throats. Why do we need to study the Matrix to be a proper for Prepper? In a word, Titanic.

WHY be a Prepper? Ask the people on the Titanic. Four Prepper lessons from the Titanic. The captain said,God can not sink this ship. The escape rafts went out half empty. Escape rafts have to get away from the massive sinking ship or be pulled under. The survivors in the water can swamp your escape raft. Some painful analogies can be drawn for modern day preppers from these factoids from the Titanic. Grasp a solar flare and you will become a prepper.

What is a solar flare? A solar flare is an explosion on the Sun. Earth is composed of wise men, simple men, fools and scorners. We are not to cast our pearls before swine or they will turn and bite us. A scorner is a fool with an attitude. Don't waste your time with endless debates with scorners. An heretic after the first or second admonition reject. I never waste more than three seconds on a scorner, but they influence the simple. So for the sake of the simple I will reach down to scorner level to make the fait accompli about EMP, CME solar flares.

Does the Sun exist? Yes. What is the Sun? A big ball of explosions. How often does the Sun have explosions? 24/7
How often does the Sun have CMEs, coronal mass ejections/solar storms? Often.What direction are these massive solar storm sprung out at? Every direction.

Is there any frequency or pattern? Yes and No. The Sun, like a drunken cowboy with two six guns gets around to shooting Earth about every 70 years according to Matthew Stein of When Technology Fails. That means CME could happen today and again in two weeks or not for another two hundred years.
When was the last time when had a coronal mass ejection CME hit he earth? The Earth is hit continuously but a massive

disabling CMEs one occurred several years ago.
What is the CMEs effect of Earth? On the low end your flight might get canceled. On the high end all flights might get canceled and your car canceled and everything else canceled. The smaller our chips get and the more dependent we are on them and the greater our ability to be thrown back to the stone age by an EMP or CME solar storm. A massive solar storm in the modern computer driven world would be devastating.

Do solar storms care about your political affiliation, national origin, gender or tendencies? No. You would be a prepper if you truly understood that with solar storms. You are but a step from death. What would happen if suddenly, blink, everything turns off and doesn't turn back on again? It would be Hurricane Sandy on a national scale lasting a long, long time.

You need to feel the Matrix or you will not properly prepare and maybe not prepare at all. There is a difference between a “Boy Scout” prepper and a “Doomsday Prepper.” There is a difference between a “Christian” prepper and a “Military Prepper.” Like Bruce Lee's Toa of Jeet Kune Do, I like to combine it all like MMA. Most prepper planning has no factoring of the number one cause of death-democide. I believe you should do worst case scenario playing first. Plan for the worst, hope for the best. Being a Boy Scout Prepper and having nice weeny roasts will do you no good when a XM1 A1 my dad built comes rumbling through your forest. About that time you wish you had been a military prepper.

Many people are in such poor condition physically that they can not run 100 yards if their life depended on it. Note to self- You may need to run a 100 yards to save your life. Many modern young people fail boot camp. Your preparations are incomplete if they are not including getting in shape. You should learn to do non-equipment calisthenic exercises.

With non-equipment exercises having no professional equipment is no excuse! Non-equipment exercises include: push ups, hip ups, bar dips, pull ups, crunches, sit ups, leg lifts, box stepper, knee dips, toe lifts, squats, stretches. You have to raise your metabolic rate to burn fat all day. Slothfulness casteth into a deep sleep. Digital scales are superior to analog scales in that they don't allow wiggle room. Being in shape is a non-negotiable for a prepper.

Why be a prepper? Natural disasters: tornadoes, hurricanes, earthquakes, blizzards, solar storms, severe thunderstorms, hurricanes, fires.

Why be a prepper? Man made disasters: chemical spills, radioactive mishaps, war, oppressive governments.

Why be a prepper? Collapse of society caused by the shortages of electricity, fuel, food, water, or financial disruption. Your masters could claim the Chinese had a invisible national level hacker attack and the government could declare a “bank holiday”. No, boys and girls Christmas is not a bank holiday. Flash mobs could start appearing in days. It would be a little late to snuggle up to a prepper manual and a warm Mocha Latte with cream. That's when people will digging through the attic for survival techniques that were scribbled on the back of C-ration boxes. Why prep? Because He said WHEN not IF.

WHEN not IF the winds come - The rain descended, and the floods came, and the winds blew, and beat upon that house; and it fell not: for it was founded upon a rock-Descendió la lluvia,vinieron ríos,soplaron vientos y golpearon contra aquella casa;pero no cayó,porque estaba cimentada sobre la roca-Als nun der Platzregen fiel und die Wasserströme kamen und die Winde stürmten und an dieses Haus stießen,fiel es nicht;denn es war auf den Felsen gegründet.

Why prep? Because dark days are coming when-no man might buy or sell, save he that had the mark-of the beast. There is nothing that says everything will be rosy up to that day.

Y que ninguno pudiera comprar ni vender, sino el que tuviera la marca o el nombre de la bestia o el número de su nombre. und dass niemand kaufen oder verkaufen kann als nur der, welcher das Malzeichen hat oder den Namen des Tieres oder die Zahl seines Namens.

Why prep? Ask why the DHS has been amassing an billions rounds of hollow point bullets. Ask why shopping malls are secured and schools are unsecured. Ask why FEMA coffins are stacked on acres of land all over the nation. Ask why WHO, the CDC, FEMA and DHS have preparations for mass casualties.

Why is it normal, rational and acceptable for the government to be working at a fever pitch for preparedness and yet they tell the sheeple to take the blue pill and go back to sleep? The media masters convince you that commoners are insane or delusional if they make any preparations. Rich people have gated communities, body guards, fortified cars, safe rooms, mountain hide outs and armed guards at their kids private schools. Yet, commoners are considered odd and extreme if they have extra cans of store-able food. Psy-ops is how the controllers get simple minded people to stand down. They call you silly and reactionary. Malcolm X said that my dad was born a suspect. People like us don't care about be the main stream and accepted by the yuppies at the cool table at the insane asylum. Don't drink the kool-aide. Don't let them convince you to be polite and go quietly into the night. Be a prepper.

To be a wise prepper you need to understand the capacities of Unmanned Aerial Vehicles (UAVs). You might want to know that UAVs can be armed and are capable of disbursing chemical or biological weapons. Drones are cute but they are not your friends. In war you need to make a clear distinguish between your friends and your enemies. To be a survivor you need to know when to hold 'em, when to fold 'em, when to walk away and when to run.

Why prep? The U.S. House of Representatives passed HR 6566 which is an amendment of the Homeland Security Act of 2002 that imbues the Administrator of the Federal Emergency Management Agency (FEMA) “to provide guidance and coordination for mass fatality planning, and for other purposes." Why?

Why prep? Samuel Adams "If ye love wealth better than liberty, the tranquility of servitude better than the animating contest of freedom, go home from us in peace. We ask not your counsels or arms. Crouch down and lick the hands which feed you. May your chains set lightly upon you, and may posterity forget that ye were our countrymen."

Why prep? Read the book-When Technology Fails by Matthew Stein. Why be a prepper? Have you ever had the lights go out? Have you ever had the heat not work? Have you ever had the water not work? What if someone trues to mug you? What if someone tries to break in your house? What if there is a riot, flood, earth quake, tornadao, hurrriacane, fire, war, plague, radiation,...?

Why prep? Visit these web sites:

www.infowars.com

www.prisonplanet.tv

www.cuttingthroughthematrix.com

www.rense.com

www.infowars.com/darpa-emergency-response-robot-runs-faster-than-usain-bolt

www.infowars.com/femas-camp-freedom-concentration-camp-with-blackhawk-helicopters-flying-above

www.cbsnews.com/8301-201_162-57547551/11-days-without-power-sandy-victims-want-answers

www.nbcnewyork.com/on-air/as-seen-on/Residents-Dumpster-Dive-in-Lower-East-Side-After-Storm_New-York.html

www.prisonplanet.com/unrest-growing-among-nj-ny-citizens-dumpster-diving-for-food-fist-fights-over-fuel-tempers-flare-in-sandy-aftermath.html

Why prep? Hear the quote: PREPPERS CREED: GOVERNMENT WILL NOT BE THERE FOR YOU IN A CRISIS. Why prep? Read the articles: Gerald Celente, Trends Research Institute "Neo-Survivalism" Pentagon Wants Packs Of Robots To Detect "Non-cooperative Humans"

- Upcoming Military Robot Could Feed on Dead Bodies
- Chemtrails that don't exist cost 5 billion a year to produce
- DARPA "Emergency Response" Robot Runs Faster Than Usain Bolt
- Military Industrial Complex Prepares Mass Graves for U.S. Citizens
- Gov't Following 'Stalinist Model' for Detaining

Veterans Under NDAA

- FEMA To Mobilize For "Mass Fatality Planning"
- Video Footage of Phoenix Mass Grave Site
- New Mexico Department Of Health Prepares For Influenza Mass Vaccination Clinics
- Plans for Mass Graves Confirmed: Government Surveying Cemetery Readiness for Flu Outbreak
- Flu Pandemic: Mass Graves and Martial Law
- Scottish Government Prepares Thousands of Cardboard Coffins for Pandemic

Why be a prepper? Watch these movies:

- Bourne Legacy
- Dark Secrets inside Bohemian Grove
- Eagle Eye
- End Game-Blue Print for global enslavement
- Enemy of the State
- Eyes Wide Shut (R-rating)
- Fall of the Republic-Alex Jones
- Hunger Games
- Idiocracy
- Manchurian Candidate
- Red Dawn (both)
- Road Warrior

- Sound of Music
- Terminator
- The Road (2009)

Why prep? Watch this YouTube: WHY IN THE WORLD ARE THEY SPRAYING?

Why prep? Hear this quote: Khrushchev said. "Your children will live under communism." "You Americans are so gullible. No, you won't accept Communism outright; but we'll keep feeding you small doses of Socialism until you will finally wake up and find that you already have Communism. We won't have to fight you; we'll so weaken your economy, until you fall like overripe fruit into our hands."

2. PREP WHO?

Who should you listen to about prepping? Prep who? Who should you listen to about prepping? Should you listen to the most eloquent or smoothest writer or best the dressed? Should you listen to the old soldier sitting on a log in the woods using a stick to draw illustrations in the dirt? Do you kill the messenger with ad hominem attacks because he speaks in the clear? Am I therefore become your enemy, because I tell you the truth. ¿Me he vuelto, por tanto, vuestro enemigo al deciros la verdad?Bin ich denn damit euer Feind geworden, daß ich euch die Wahrheit vorhalte?

Prep who? Its not deception for the enemy to wear his uniform, it's deception for the enemy to wear YOUR uniform. Be discerning about to whom you listen because Satan can transform himself into an angel of light.

Prep who? Be careful WHO you partner with. Find and develop good partners not someone who has or will back stab a someone in family court. If people threw there “loved” ones under the bus in the best of times you are a fool to think they wouldn't turn on you in real hard times hit and things turn road warrior. My father was loyal to his troops and his family when bullets were flying and times were really hard. He did not lose or abandon any of his troops in his specific unit. In fact, he he got a medal for making himself a human shield. Even to this day my elderly dad will ask me if the troops are OK. He also always asks about his grankids and says he doesn't want anything to happen to mom. Dad does not realize moms is with Jesus now, she's going to be OK.

Prep who? Who should you listen to. Honor the grey head. My father taught me to listen to OLD soldiers in country that are alive, and are going home as survivors. Seek the old parhs. Some young bucks disrespect the aged. Note they consider anyone with a couple of gray hairs aged. They try to rib me. I tell them when they are my age they will be dead. Physican heal thyself. Prove your Kung Fu by surviving. I have seen many laid low needlessly. I have seen a lot of wreckage of society. Your parents had high hopes for you, but your life ended face down in a poodle, in a dark alley over a ten dollar dope deal. "Who" to talk to about preparedness? Talk to survivors.

Prep who? Listen to speaker Dr. Doug Rokke: The Dangers of Using Depleted Uranium.

Prep who? Listen to speaker: Joel Skousen on strategic relocation.

Prep who? Read Jim Rawles, survivalist author. A former Intelligence officer and technical writer.

Prep who? Visit the web site www.SurvivalBlog.com

Prep who? Listen to speaker: Stewart

Prep who? Listen to speakers:

For information on health-My Health teachers on youTube: Dr. Joel Wallach, Dr. Leonard Coldwell, Dr. Russell Blaylock, Dr. Mayer Eisenstein, Dr. Gary Null, Dr. Joseph Mercola, Dr. Len Horowitz, Dr. Ron Paul, Dr. Rand Paul, Dr. Peter Glidden, Dr. Sherri Tenpenny, Dr. David Hartsuch, Pharmacist Ben Fuchs and Health Ranger-Mike Adams.

Prep who? Listen to speakers:
My Spiritual teachers on youTube: Pastor Schlagl, Pastor Kurt Skelly, Pastor Stringer, J Vernon McGee, Ravi Zacharias, Frank Turek, Ken Ham, Dr. Duane Gish, David Jeremiah, Pastor Chuck Baldwin.

Prep who? Listen to speakers:
My academic teachers on YouTube: Financial Analysts-Max Keiser, Peter Schiff, Jim Rogers, Marc Faber, Gerald Celente, Alex Jones, Webster Tarpley, Porter Stanberry, Catherine Austin Fitts, Bob Chapman.

3. PREP WHAT?

Prep what? Grub-Dr Joel Wallach is a great man. You should

have him tell you why animals prefer muddy water.

Prep what? Prepare what? Prepare your body, soul and spirit. Get in shape. Get your finances in order. Try to get your interpersonal relationships right. Get your mind right. Don't fog your brain on aspartame, fluoride and booze. You will need all your facilities at maximum potential to survive. Prepare your body, soul and spirit like you are preparing for a UFC fight or the Olympics. Gerald Celente says, get it all in shape: body, soul and spirit.

4. PREP WHEN?

Prep when? Prep NOW! Prep when? Hey USMC Brandon Raub, Thank you for your service, now lock up! The sweeps and purges have begun. Detained Marine's attorney said, I am getting calls from vets all over the country. People everywhere are getting picked up.

NdAA is now in effect. NdAA is gitmo for everyone. Watch the movie: Rendition.

Prep when? Being a prepper is all about advanced planning. Anne Frank taught us a hard lesson about waiting too long. The opposite of the Sound of Music story where they got out of Dodge. Just like Curious George escaped from Paris on bicycle as Hitler marched in.

Prep when? Now. Having eyes they see not. It is natural to man to indulge in the illusions of hope. We are apt to shut our eyes against a painful truth. I am willing to know the whole truth- and to provide for it.

Prep when? Prep now. Excuses can't make the clock stop ticking. The days of our years are 70-Los días de nuestra edad son setenta años-Unser Leben währt siebzig Jahre- and if by reason of strength-80.

Prep when? He also that is slothful in his work is brother.
Prep when? Americans are leaving the U.S. in record numbers. More U.S. citizens than ever before are living outside of the country. 6.4 million Americans are either working or studying overseas, which Gallup says is the largest number ever for such statistic. When the smart rich people are loading their wagons and getting out of Dodge you might want to find out why. Gross point was filled with for sale signs.

Prep when? Everyone has the same 24 hours, the question is what we do with it.

Prep when? Prep in the "summer". The ants are a people not strong, yet they prepare their meat in the summer;
Die Ameisen, ein schwaches Volk; dennoch schaffen sie im Sommer ihre Speise, las hormigas, pueblo sin fuerza, que preparan su alimento en el verano.

Prep when? Prep early. My mentor said to me, I never lost any money by being early, but I've lost a lot being late.

Prep when? A close call to a wise man is a warning. A close call to a fool is just a close call.

Prep when? What time is it? It's late. As it was in the days of Noah so shall it be in the day of the coming of the son of man. We're even gene splicing like the antediluvian-s did. They were eating and drinking unto the day the Noah entered into the Ark and the flood sweep them all away.

Prep when? SANDY WAS A WAKE UP CALL. Hurricane Sandy taught self assured, confident New Yorkers how quickly tempers can flare. It taught us the thin veneer of civil society can wash away with just three days of rain. Sandy said, BE A PREPPER or be hungry, cold and in the dark, waiting for the gabbment to save you.

Millions of wealthy Amerikans suffered with no food, no water, no gas, no electricity for electronic food stamp debit cards or other cards. Suddenly, BINK, the lights go out now you can live with what ever you have in your pockets for the next week or so.

In New York they were dumpster diving for food and fighting over fuel in only three days after Hurricane Sandy. Many cell phones and gas stations were not working at all. Store shelves were quickly emptied and people were searching for batteries. Police had to guard the few gas stations that were working to stave off riots. Formerly vilified preppers were vindicated.

Emergency services were not able to handle a city the size of New York. Self reliance was the word of the day for the domesticated addled masses.

Many people were not fit to walk and most people did not own bicycles. We are used to knocking people around the world back to the stone age, now we are sitting in the dark and cold. Hurricane Sandy was a wake up call for people to become preppers. A close call to a wise man is a warning. A close call to a fool is just a close call. Most New Yorkers ignored all the warnings about a coming storm. We have 24 hour news and smart phones in the hands of not so smart people. Have we learned? Are we humbled?

Hurricane Sandy left millions in NYC left without electricity, no water, no toilets, no cash, no transportation. It left them with looters and sewers backing up. It had them dumpster diving. It had people turning hallways into toilets.

Hurricane Sandy showed us that the governments answer was FEMA's Camp Freedom. Camp Freedom looked like a concentration camp with people freezing in unheated tents. It was set-up by FEMA at Monmouth Park in Oceanport, New Jersey. Sheeple were coxed into going there with promises of washing machines and hot showers. Others were offered the comfort of a prison cell. Many were just stuck in the apartments watching their children getting cold. All the lame excuses in the world didn't warm those kids or fill their bellies. What a wake up call!

Prep when? Visit web site: www.tinyurl.com/sweeps-n-purges
Prep when? www.bit.ly/survivalist-sawyer-broadcast

Prep when? Visit web site:

www.youtube.com/watch?v=wQC0e9E-KSs

Prep when? Listen to quote by: Aleksandr Solzhenitsyn, in the Gulag Archipelago, How We Burned In The Camps

Prep when? Visit web site: The best news site to listen to www.Infowars.com

5. PREP WHERE

Prep where? The best author on WHERE to relocation is Joel Skousen.

Prep where? Visit this web site: www.tinyurl.com/prepper-relocate

Prep where? Visit this web site:

www.prisonplanet.com/strategic-relocation-the-film-full-version-hq.html

6. PREP HOW? How to prep

Prep how? Most people don't think and the people that think they think do not think well. You must labor to have clear thoughts when it comes to being a prepper. So much mind fog, so much be preconditioning to overcome.

Prep how? If the devil can't make you bad he will make you

busy. It is easy to turn to the left or the right and not set your face as flint toward proper preparedness. Salute no man in the way.

Prep how? Study Bob Safford's Millionaire University

Prep how? Read Susanne Posel's blog OccupyCorporatism.com.

Prep how? Visit web site:
www.marcandangel.com/2012/01/22/12-things-successful-people-do-differently

Prep how? Learn: Why is it important to learn 500 infowar terms?

Prep how? If you go with the flow the flow leads to the sewer. The road to Hell is broad and traveled by many. Why would you be yearning to follow the crowd?

Prep how? Read: Top 10 Tips For Getting Started Prepping By Jan Kelly-Thursday March 29, 2012

Prep how? Read: 12 Things That We Can Learn From Hurricane Irene About How To Prepare For Disasters And Emergencies

Prep how? Visit web site:

www.AmericanPreppersNetwork.com

Prep how? Goal oriented. Stretching-ly realistic measurable metrics.

The difference between a goal and a dream is a goal has a dead line. Bob Safford's Millionaire University said the difference between poor people and rich people is poor people don't manage their time (or anything else). Bob taught us that successful people are daily goal setters and daily goal hitters. Accountability partners help. Find someone with heart, brains and guts. J. Paul Morgan said you have to find partners because we are bond by time and space. Two are better than one. Woe unto to him that is alone when he falleth for he hath not another to lift him up. A three fold cord is not easily broken. For planning I prefer horizontal full year wall calendars procured from office supply stores. I have also learned not to make MY goals dependent on other people. As a prepper I am busting my spleen to achieve my preparedness goals in a timely manner. It is frustrating to fail with a big goose egg zero at the end of a full year because I am waiting on someone else. Once you realize how much prepper work you have to do, you don't want to want to be overwhelmed and stop. Major on the majors and minor on the minors. A Japanese business man friend of mine said he had a hard time expressing what a drop dead dead line means.

It is so easy to get sidetracked on your prepper goals. Salute no man in the way. Don't turn to the left or to the right. Set your face as flint toward the goal. A famous proverb: How do you eat an elephant? One bite at a time. By the inch it's a cinch. NOTE-Preparedness is all about advance planning. When the situation hits the fan you don't want to be way behind the power curve. Once the grid goes down prepper efforts go from simple to very very difficult. Being a prepper is not a spectacular sport. You can't hire people to exercise for you. God said, knowledge would increase but He did not say that wisdom would increase. There have been and will continue to be well educated rich people rolled up in old rugs lying on the side of the streets when disaster strikes. Research on Vesuvius indicates that rich people burn just and fast as poor people.

Being busy in a rocking chair doesn't move you down the road. The hand of the diligent shall bear rule, but you should sharpen the ax before you use it. Being a full spectrum prepper you will find to be quite a big project. Soon you will realize you have big holes in your written preparedness plan.

Seek first the kingdom of God and all these things will be added to you. Let everything be done decently and and in order. You always have time for what you put first. Preparedness is a big nut to crack. It will require diligence and forethought and focus. Don't trust the voices in your heard. Find good partners to use as sounding boards and bounce your preparedness ideas off of them. Don't weary yourself talking to "weeds", they will just wear you done. They also will be the first ones to come knocking on your door when the grid goes down. NOTE – The grid has gone down before. The grid will go down again. The question is not the grid. The question is will you be prepared? Don't sacrifice the permanent on the alter of the eternal. David behaved himself wisely, be wise. If you run preparedness drills you can detect holes in your program. In the military they are called mobilization exercises. On a micro-level I learned from my father to have a daily task list and a ten ten list to answer to by the end of the day. Every man shall give an account of himself. Walk circumspectly not as fools.

My commander said if it costs a million dollars to make a secret room 99 percent sound proof and it costs a thousand times more to make it 100 percent sound proof. You have reached the point of diminishing returns. Don't be obsessive.

F.I.D.O. Forget It and Drive On.

You need points on the score board BEFORE the two minute drill. Be wise in your preparedness, there is a clock ticking. Everyone always asks, when? No man knows the day or the hour. Everyday is one day closer, be ready. Do the worst can scenarist planning first. Make your peace with God, that is your ultimate escape plan. Hear Clutch, “Stand up, eject, escape from the prison planet.” All your unprepared neighbors are volunteering to be your cover. Eighty percent of Amerikans don't have passports, thank them before you leave.

Set stretching-ly realistic goals but don't over whelm your self and get disenchanted. You must maintain a hopeful attitude. The joy of the Lord is my strength. Wherefore lift up the hands which hang down, and the feeble knees. Keep thine heart with all diligence for out of it are the issues of life.

Breaking inertia is the hardest thing to do. Safford taught us a Millionaire University that it takes half the rocket fuel just to get off the ground. You don't “start” a preparedness project, you launch it.

Any fool can spit out excuses like a Pez dispenser, but kids eat food but they don't eat excuses. Preparedness for kids is exponentially harder. Infants eat ever two hours and defecate every two hours and it's not the same two hours. The number one cause of death of kids is diarrhea from dirty water. I know you love your kids if you buy them a Life Straw. The maximum effective range of an excuse is zero. Yes sir, no sir and no excuse sir. Kids will say, I'm hungry. You can give them your lame excuse why your weren't a prepper and they will tell you again, “I'm hungry.”

Champions and achievers function in the realm of pain. NOTE: It is cold on both sides of the football field. Cowboy up and get your preparedness program going. Opportunity is an ever closing window. Time and tide wait for no man. There comes a time when no man can work. Work for the night cometh when no man can work.

I used to be motivated for freedom, now I'm motivated for survival, there is a difference. Don't go with the flow, the flow leads to the sewer. The road to Hell is broad and traveled by many. My special forces green beret sniper martial arts instructor taught me that you must steel yourself to the fact that most people won't survive.

Use the KISS principle in preparedness. Keep It Simple and Smile. Don't show the consumer more than three pairs of shoes: good, better, best. No math on this test. Don't needlessly complicate your preparedness plan. Simplify and multiply. Some will, some won't so what, next! Make your plan idiot proof, make it G.I. proof. Gentleman this is a football, chase the guys in the wrong colored uniforms.

Watch out for the spin moves. My evangelist Jerry Johnston said, It is not deception for the enemy to wear his uniform. It is deception for the enemy to wear YOUR uniform. If you don't understand psy-ops and false flags you will not be a survivor. Most war is not physical, it's psy-op. Stalin did not physically shot 20 million people in the head. He got millions to go along with his psy-op deception as an ox goeth to the slaughter.

If you do a practice drill with your preparedness plan and it doesn't work, step back for ten and punt. The definition of insanity is doing the same thing over and over again and expecting different results. Fools have pride of authorship, they will ride their bad idea to the grave, don't join them. Shot, move and communicate. Constantly reevaluate.

Seek advice on your plan. There is safety in a multitude of

counselors. With much counsel make war. Don't sit in a corner and mumble to yourself. Your preparedness it is a matter of life and death for you and your loved ones.

I count my successes incrementally or I would be despondent. Understand delta force principle. It is better to get 10,000 troops there in 3 days rather than 100,000 troops there in a month. Get a hasty plan put together and then continuously upgrade it like your life depended on it.

Try to form a team. One person can only produce one persons output. A team of two has more synergy and can produce 2.4.

I am big on charts, graphs, digital scales and analog watches. I can feel my preparedness progress when I see my analog charts. No fudge factor in digital scales. There is no end of tweaking. Constantly up your game. Be brutally honest with yourself.

Self employed people don't need a boss to yell at them. In preparedness planning you need to be in self-employed mode.

The world is filled with variables and constants. Control all the constants, variables I can not control. Roll with the variables.

Don't expect what you don't inspect. Don't fear making a mistake. Fear is a snare unto a man. Malcolm X said, we don't

want to make our people sad. Sad people don't do anything. We want to get you mad. Survival-ism is an attitude. My father out survived his enemies.
It is difficult to find good prepper partners. Leonardo da Vinci said, If you want to travel fast, travel alone. I believe it was Rawles who said, He that travels alone travels fastest, but he that travels as a team travels farthest.

He that walks with wise men shall be wise but a companion of fools shall be destroyed. Don't hang out with fools. Watch out for cointel. If you don't understand cointel, you will be spending plenty of quality time with people who can explain it to you. Most dissenters are just mocking birds and useful idiots, but there are paid agent provocateurs and change agents. If you don;t understand these terms plan on getting a bloody nose.

Work hard on you preparedness but rest. God says, Come apart and rest for a while (or you will just come apart). Honor your Sabbath rest principle, the French learned if you ignore it, you will be reminded the hard way, ask their mules.

People think in the back of their mind that they would survive if the grid went down. Reality is the average person would only survive a few days in the wild or in a apocalyptic scenario. Most people "got no" fight game. Go to an MMA gym, sign the liability release, step into the cage and learn how feeble you really are, humbling. Go camping in a tent on the ground in the snow and get a reality check as to how woefully unprepared you really are, frightening.

What is a man profiteth if he gains the whole world and loses his soul. Deal with the supernatural, philosophical preparedness. Another constraint in your prepper plan is trying to help your family. If any man provide not for his own especially those of his own house he has defied the faith and is worse than an infidel. Sometimes the best way to help your hard headed family is to move ahead with your preparedness and hope they come running in time when the grid goes down. Goebbels said, eventually even the thickest of people will look out the window and the media propaganda will not hold up. The only question is will there be any time left on their clock.
If the devil can't make you bad he'll make you busy. Don't get side tracked from your preparedness plans. I recommend Jesus, the Master Prepper.

PART TWO-LEARN FROM THE BEST PREPPER

(CHAPTER-Christian Prepper Chapter Mark 13)

1 VERSE: And as He went out of the temple, one of His disciples saith unto Him, Master, see what manner of stones and what buildings are here!

1 REMARK: People are impressed with the sophistication of society. People think that because there is so much technology that we could never collapse. The Mings were conquered by the less sophisticated Mongols. Trends Researcher Gerald Celente eloquently bemoaned the conquest of the barbaric Nazis over the civilized Germans; the Romans over the more sophisticated Greeks. People think that because of all the pretty shiny things we have that surely this could not all be swept away. Lebanon was a tourist resort rivaling Hawaii. Lebanon was bombed back to the stone age. People arrogantly think, oh that could never happen here. History and reality simply don't support people's pampered presumptions.

2 VERSE: And Jesus answering said unto him, Seest thou these great buildings? there shall not be left one stone upon another, that shall not be thrown down.

2 REMARK: Jesus is taking the long view of history. Jesus sees through history and sees the people scattered like sheep without a shepherd. Elisha wept when he foresaw that Hazael would slaughter the woman and children. A wise man seeth danger afar off. The people of Jeremiah's day said, prophecy

unto us smooth things, prophecy unto us deceits. Wise mature people will hear the worst of it and adjust their game as the founding fathers said. Hey doc, tell it to me straight. Valuable time and resources are wasted by people wanting some one to rub their ears with comfy words that don't change the harsh reality barreling down the highway at them.

3 VERSE: And as He sat upon the mount of Olives over against the temple, Peter and James and John and Andrew asked Him privately,

3 Remark: From years of being verbally beat up many people are embarrassed to ask questions publicly. I tell rookies ten percent of people are severely damaged. Don't ask them questions. Don't make eye contact, just walk away. Another ten percent of the people are cool. Ask them a million questions...while you are a rookie. When it comes to preparedness ten percent of the people will say you are crazy, just trust the gabbament. Just walk away from those people, don't make eye contact. With it hits the fan they will be the first ones pushing you out of the way to dumpster dive looking for scraps of molded food. Another ten percent of the population are cool. They may not even be preppers but they can teach you to make fire or tie a square knot. In the age of smarter phones and dumber people the data is literally sitting in your hand. A lazy man will not so much as raise his hand to his mouth. You can lead people to water but you can not make them think. If you don't know something in this information age then you just simply don't want to know. Jesus said, be careful HOW you hear. God said that knowledge would increase, but He did not say that wisdom would increase.

4 VERSE: Tell us, when shall these things be? and what shall be the sign when all these things shall be fulfilled?

4 REMARK: People always ask others and myself, "When will it be?" Human nature is to procrastinate. People are naturally slugs. Slugs will get you killed. Jesus said they were eating and drinking to the DAY that Noah entered into the Ark. Fight your natural urge to wait and procrastinate. Understand that every day is one day closer to the guaranteed prophecy of the super Nazi anti-Christ, where no man will buy or sell without the mark of the beast. Wise people can see the control grid tightening up a little more everyday. I believe that God can give us a reprieve like Nineveh but they were eventually destroyed. I do not trouble myself about things beyond my pay grade. I simply do what is within the scope of my ability and responsibility. If I fail and die, that's OK. If I perish, I perish. I know in whom I have believed in and am persuaded that He is able to keep that which I have committed unto Him. Make your peace with God BEFORE the fire fight starts. I tell the rookies when something happens you have literally one, maybe 2 seconds to react. You can not react that fast without having thought things through and reduced them to muscle memory. Three, four seconds, that's too late. It's the quick and the dead.

5 VERSE: And Jesus answering them began to say, Take heed lest any man deceive you:

5 REMARK: Satan is a deceiver. Most animals have camouflage. They use spin, smoke and mirrors to sneak up on their prey. A jaguar can't run fast, but it can crawl like a blanket on the ground to within fifteen feet of his prey. Christians above everyone should have discernment and should be looking for the spin. When I talk to a criminal, I don't expect a criminal to act like any thing other than a criminal. I expect him to lie. How do you know a politician is lying, their lips are moving. Why would anyone expect truth from corporately owned media. Eighty percent of poison is perfectly edible. You have to mix poison in with a lot of truth for it to sell. Many

people are terminally naive. Sheeple get eaten. When there is a disaster I expect some paid clown pressitute to get on the TV and calm the crowd “for their safety”. I don't care what that clown says, I am getting out of Dodge. Rather safe than sorry. You don't want to be on the last train out. You want to out on the train BEFORE the last train out. I don't care if I leave town a head of the hurricane every year, so what. A super high end CPA told me you can do one hundred good real estate deals and do fine. You can have one bad real estate deal and lose everything you have ever owned in a life time. You can have one bad hurricane or tornado and everything you own can be scattered for twenty miles. One “good” fire and all you baby pictures are gone forever. You may want to put them to DVD and a cloud. Learn to discern what can not be replaced. You will be overwhelmed trying to carry that which is replaceable and lose that which is irreplaceable.

6 VERSE: For many shall come in my name, saying, I am Christ; and shall deceive many.

6 REMARK: Key words “deceive many”. Most people are not going to make it. The road to Hell is broad and traveled by many. The biggest psy-op for groupie sheeple is the appeal to be accepted by the group. If you follow the flow the flow leads to the sewer. Everyone stampedes each other to death for the same fire exit. Step back, be cool and walk quietly through the exit no one is heading toward.

7 VERSE: And when ye shall hear of wars and rumours of wars, be ye not troubled: for such things must needs be; but the end shall not be yet.

7 REMARK: I tell my men that you have only so much emotional pathos in your canteen. Do not wear yourself out shadow boxing. Rookie officers wear themselves out gunning

their engines. Learn to throttle down. Take you physical and mental sabbath. Jesus said. "Come apart and rest for a while" (or you will just come apart). The number one cause of disease is stress. Stop wearing yourself out beating the air. If by reason of STRENGTH 80.

8 VERSE- For nation shall rise against nation, and kingdom against kingdom: and there shall be earthquakes in divers places, and there shall be famines and troubles: these are the beginnings of sorrows.

8-REMARK-Are these not preparedness issues: wars, earthquakes, famines? Christians above everyone should live with these realities. They should structure their affairs accordingly. It is the blind world-lings that dwell in cities without walls. Sheeple defy history and current reality that every state has declared a state of emergency. The rulers want the sheeple to be docile and dependent on the state. They hate rugged individualism. They hate Amish selling beans on the side of the road. They only give lip service to wanting to help the self-employed. Don't go by the lovely speeches and brochures. Look at their tax policies. Ask yourself, Why are they raiding kid's lemonade stands?

9 VERSE: But take heed to yourselves: for they shall deliver you up to councils; and in the synagogues ye shall be beaten: and ye shall be brought before rulers and kings for my sake, for a testimony against them.

9 REMARK: Take heed. You will endure legal assaults. You will be sued. You should adjust your world accordingly. That is an element of preparedness that I have never heard anyone talk about. What silliness to talk about preparedness and not address that fact that you live in the most litigious country on the planet. Don't worry about a fire stealing everything for

which you worked to attain. You will never hear mentioned that the greatest amount of litigation is "family" law. You can do all the preparedness you want to and come home to a house that has been robbed from the inside. No jury, no rules of evidence and no punishment for perjury. You are not doing anyone any favors by being too polite to talk about the real threats in life. Twenty years of hard labor gone instantly, with the stroke of a pen by a kangaroo court and a lying, back stabbing Judas. All through history peons and peasants have been rustled up before bogus courts and stripped of all their worldly possessions by some grand inquisitor on a straw throne with a tin crown. Do not the rich men oppress you and draw you before the judgment seats.

10 VERSE: And the gospel must first be published among all nations.

10 REMARK: The Word of God can NOT be bound, this gives me hope. Many silk pants people constantly ask me to put a happy face on this bloody mess. Here is my hope-Jesus. God is stronger than the boogie man. THY kingdom come. THY will be done. Every knee SHALL bow and EVERY tongue shall confess that Jesus Christ is Lord. It seems like the "elite" have total power. No! GOD stops them cold at certain points. Many times these that make the world to tremble, die very ignominious deaths with dung smeared in their face Malachi says. God allows free will. Criminals think they can run wild and do what they want. Criminals live in a dream. When they cross the wrong line the order goes out. Go get them and bring them back in a bag or chains. No concern for cost and effort, go get them. So likewise with these "elite" who think they can get away with everything. No. God will drive a nail through their foot. God told Satan you can do what you want to Job, but do NOT kill him. Satan is as wild as the come but even he has boundaries God will not let him cross. The

robber barons and banksters that have destroyed our world. They think the music will never end. I assure the death angels does need a hall pass to get past security in Aspen.

11 VERSE: But when they shall lead you, and deliver you up, take no thought beforehand what ye shall speak, neither do ye premeditate: but whatsoever shall be given you in that hour, that speak ye: for it is not ye that speak, but the Holy Ghost.

11 REMARK: You can spend a million dollars and make every effort for ten years to build the ultimate survival plan and you can still catch a stray bullet. The warrior king disguised himself, yet a certain man drew his bow at a venture, and smote the king-between the joints of the armor. Anyone can accidentally step in front of a bus. Anyone can get delivered up to corrupt authorities. That's why you have to make your peace with God ahead of time. Develop your eternal exit strategy first. I am able to talk about preparedness issues because I have the hope of Heaven. If I did not, I would constantly be playing reindeer games in my head about how everything is going to be OK, just go back to sleep. Cognitive dissonance is a coping mechanism for people who do have a real answer for the certainty of death and the horrors of life.

12 VERSE: Now the brother shall betray the brother to death, and the father the son; and children shall rise up against their parents, and shall cause them to be put to death.

12 REMARK: Despite the TV shows glamorizing court room drama the reality is the number one litigation in law is “family” court. America is number one in divorce and prisons. The highest probability is you be attacked by your own family in “family” kangaroo court. I have conducted extensive efforts in family law reform. Family court is the number one threat to your finances. Everything you have studied for in school and

college; everything you have worked for in your career or business -washed away with no trial, no jury, no rules of evidence, no perjury protection. It is not by accident, it is by design. Julius Caesar destroyed the families after the battle of Gaul. The communist and the Illuminati said, before you can destroy the country you must destroy the family. President Johnson destroyed the Black community with the stroke of a pen. Slaves had their families constantly disrupted. It is a means of control. Brace for impact. An ounce of prevention is worth a pound of cure. You will not be able to protect your kids if they are stolen from you. Half of all marriages end in divorce. Half of all dads will never see their kids again. What preparedness plan do you have for kids you never see? How well are the females going to protect the kids from a failed state with rioters running up and down the streets with torches? People live a dream that they have a fight game, but most people couldn't last 60 seconds in a UFC cage. Once the family is shattered it's everyman for himself. Where will the corrupt "family" court judges be with a Road Warrior society as depicted in the 2009 movie called the Road?

Recommended-sites:
www.anthonyhtaylor.legalshield.com
www.fathers-4-justice.org
www.f4j.com
www.iowafathers.com
www.illinoisfathers.org
www.dadsofmichigan.blogspot.com
www.AcFc.org

13 VERSE: And ye shall be hated of all men for my name's sake: but he that shall endure unto the end, the same shall be saved.

13 REMARK: Some disaster scenarios seem hopeless but God

says, some will survive. Ye shall be hated. The endless drum beat of conformity training is to be “popular”. Soon after elementary school people should break the “popularity” conditioning.

14 VERSE: But when ye shall see the abomination of desolation, spoken of by Daniel the prophet, standing where it ought not, (let him that readeth understand,) then let them that be in Judaea flee to the mountains:

14 REMARK: Flee to the mountains. Run for the hills. Why mountains? David was able to hide in the hills for years against an army.

15 VERSE: And let him that is on the housetop not go down into the house, neither enter therein, to take any thing out of his house:

15 REMARK: B.O.B. Bug Out Bag. In emergencies seconds count. Minutes can be the difference between life an death. In a hurricane you have three days to get ready. In a tornado you have 60 seconds to get ready, there is a difference. Have a duplicate of everything you need in your B.O.B.. It is quite a contest to keep the B.O.B. weight down and not freeze. Study ultra light gear. Have a BOB for your car and for your house.

16 VERSE: And let him that is in the field not turn back again for to take up his garment.

16 REMARK: An O.R.P. is an Organizational Rallying Point. Warn your crew and then head to the ORP. Wait a reasonable amount of time. Assume that they are not coming and roll out. That is a hard move, but necessary.

17 VERSE: But woe to them that are with child, and to them that give suck in those days!

17 REMARK: I can move a hundred troops faster than a woman with a baby. Babies don't far well in battle. The number one causality in war is kids. Kids can't defend themselves. Kids can't handle the elements. A thirty pound child can not hold heat as well as a two hundred and twenty five pound man. The number one cause of death for kids is diarrhea from dirty water. How do I know that you understand and love your children? You will have a forty dollar portable water filter. You should send your child away when you hear a run up. You can always claw your way out if things go hot.

18 VERSE: And pray ye that your flight be not in the winter.

18 REMARK: How long will a multi-million person city above the Latitude freeze line survive when the grid goes down?

19 VERSE: For in those days shall be affliction, such as was not from the beginning of the creation which God created unto this time, neither shall be.

19 REMARK: How much affliction can the average soft suburbanite endure? American soldiers use six times as much pain medicine as foreign soldiers. One in four females use psychotropic drugs. The average old person is on a dozen drugs. If you are serious about preparedness and survivalism you may want to tighten your shot group.

20 VERSE: And except that the Lord had shortened those days, no flesh should be saved: but for the elect's sake, whom he hath chosen, he hath shortened the days.

20 REMARK: God is King forever. Thy Kingdom come. Thy

will be done. I read the last chapter- God wins in the end. Join the winning team. Whosoever shall call upon the name of the Lord shall be saved.

21 VERSE: And then if any man shall say to you, Lo, here is Christ; or, lo, he is there; believe him not:

21 REMARK: False run ups wore down Jericho. People get mentally fatigued and numb. Most warfare is psy-op psychological, that is why it is critical to have a strong theological base. It is also valuable to be a serious infowarrior. There are over five hundred terms that alternative media uses that average sheeple would have no clue as to what infowarriors are talking about. What is: Gladio, false flag, ajax, northwoods, building 7, gleiwitz, gmo, chemtrail, cdo, neocon, pressitute, Bohemian grove, Bilderberg, round table, Agenda 21, agent provocateur, full spectrum dominance, cointel, Hegelian Dialectic, …? If you don't know these terms you can pack the best BOB in the world but you won't know where to go. All dressed up and no where to go. False Christs, false leaders and false flags will have you running around in circles until you collapse from exhaustion. A beaver can wear out and drown a dog by swimming backwards. I wish preparedness was simply a matter of a long camping trip i.e. boy scout prepper.

22 VERSE: For false Christs and false prophets shall rise, and shall shew signs and wonders, to seduce, if it were possible, even the elect.

22 REMARK: Christians above everyone should see through the matrix. In fact, you wouldn't be a Christian if you wouldn't have seen through the matrix. The heart is deceitful above all things. How is it fools say trust in your heart, "let your corrupt conscience be your guide?" Christians should be constantly tearing down the wizards curtains like Toto. The ruling elite

are terrified that the sleeping giant of the church will wake up. That's why many churches have been co-opted. Alex Jones points out that the church is one force that would be a game changer. If my people which are called by My name shall humble themselves and pray. I will heal their land. Ultimately we are in a supernatural battle. Puny pathetic politicians and their beards will not save us.

23 VERSE: But take ye heed: behold, I have foretold you all things.

23 REMARK: Job said, would that my enemy had written a book. Hitler did write a book. He detailed enough of his war plan. Perhaps it might have been a good idea to read his book. Mindless people try to debate me about the elite. The elite have witten a book. They foretold in writing what they are going to do and have done. If you don't know, it's because you don't want to know. You must have more important things to do, like sorting your sock drawer. When you think you see the sun coming up at two in the morning maybe it will dawn on you: A: That's not the Sun. B: Maybe I should have been a little more informed. When you have that unexpected heart attack or car wreck and you are suddenly launched into eternity all the couldda, wouldda and shouldda means nothing. The rich man thought he had the world by the tail and God said, Thou fool THIS night your soul is required of thee.

24 VERSE: But in those days, after that tribulation, the sun shall be darkened, and the moon shall not give her light,

24 REMARK: What prepper plan do you have for the sun turning off? Seek first the kingdom of God. You are not ready to live until you are ready to die. M.B.O. Manage by objective. Take care of the ultimate issue first, your soul. Everything after that is academic. How much will you sell your eyes for? How

much would you sell your soul for? What is a man profiteth if he gains the whole world and loses his soul? The reason true Christians can talk about prepper issues without batting an eye is we have a city whose Builder and Maker is God. The worst thing thing will happen to us is that we will die and go to Heaven.

25 VERSE: And the stars of heaven shall fall, and the powers that are in heaven shall be shaken.

REMARK-Prepper this! What politician can save you from this? Many people are concerned about a civilization ending meteor. Again, I submit to you a star meteor called Wormwood is way beyond your pay grade. Your beloved politicians can not save you from meteor stars falling. If you wake up looking a two hundred mile wide meteor crater that used to be your hometown, then you hopefully realize that seeking God is the only prudent option. Wise men still seek Him.

26 VERSE: And then shall they see the Son of man coming in the clouds with great power and glory.

26 REMARK: That is my hope-Jesus. No king but King Jesus. Politicians become corrupt. Governments become corrupt. Power corrupts, absolute power corrupt absolutely. Only Jesus can same us. Societies go from rags, to riches to ruin. Societies collapse under their own decadence. Jesus is the only hope. There is no other name under heaven given to men, whereby we must be saved.

27 VERSE: And then shall he send his angels, and shall gather together his elect from the four winds, from the uttermost part of the earth to the uttermost part of heaven.

27 REMARK: “Angels?” Angels and fallen angels. I was

raised in the Schwarzwald, the Black Forest. Angels and demons are a hard reality for me. Commoners may claim to be irreligious, but your Occult Aristocracy are deeply religious. Google "Illuminati images in movies" in Movies. You will never understand the urgency of preparedness until you understand the depths of evil in which your wonderful leaders are involved. For example Hell Fire Clubs as depicted in movies like Eyes Wide Shut. The silver tongue politician's dulcet tones put you to sleep with a warm glass of GMO milk and sweet promises. You would not sleep so soundly without a preparedness program if you realized the wild frat party your leaders are engaged in at that same hour. I always ask people who their state and federal level congressmen and senators are, most people don't know. These wonderful politicians you vote for and pay for are going to parties that would make Caligula blush. Sheeple think these party animals and their beards are spending every waking moment thinking of how they can save you from thermal nuclear collapse, I trow not. You better make you own Plan B-preparedness plan.

28 VERSE: Now learn a parable of the fig tree; When her branch is yet tender, and putteth forth leaves, ye know that summer is near:

28 REMARK: People think the Bible has no pictures. No, the Bible is full of pictures. Summer, fall, winter, we should learn from these cycles. Make your preparations in “summer” or starve in time of harvest. The ants are a people not strong but he prepare their meat in the summer. Develop your preparedness program now, the really bad times have not hit yet.

29 VERSE: So ye in like manner, when ye shall see these things come to pass, know that it is nigh, even at the doors.

29 REMARK: Learn to see the trends. A wise man seeth a danger a far off and hideth himself the foolish go on and are punished. See. See a far off. Recognize danger. Hide yourself or suffer the consequences. Preparedness is all about accessing the threat and making provisions for it...in advance!

30 VERSE: Verily I say unto you, that this generation shall not pass, till all these things be done.

30 REMARK: Every generation faces challenges. It is complete delusion to think that we will get a pass. Dream on if you think our wonderful politicians love us and they will take care of everything. Sheeple are utterly blind. Sheeple get eaten.

31 VERSE: Heaven and earth shall pass away: but my words shall not pass away.

31 REMARK: God's word is sure. Let God be true and every man a liar. As Nixon said, World-lings believe whatever stumbles across a TV set or whatever the "experts" say. Christians should believe whatever God says. Bad data produces bad preparedness. Vigilant preppers should have a reflex action of shelling through data looking for truth.

32 VERSE: But of that day and that hour knoweth no man, no, not the angels which are in heaven, neither the Son, but the Father.

32 REMARK: Duct tape this verse to your TV. How many charlatans come bouncing across they TV screen saying that they know the "day and the hour". They numb people to the reality that one day it will be game on. Whether you plan and live with the reality or not there is an end to you, your country, your world. The things that are seen are temporary, the things that are unseen are eternal.

33 VERSE: Take ye heed, watch and pray: for ye know not when the time is.

33 REMARK: Ye know NOT the time. Ye know NOT the time. Ye know NOT the time. The price of freedom is eternal vigilance. Watch. Be informed. Be engaged. WATCH does not mean sitting in a corner staring at a wall. People pride themselves about the fact that they don't know anything about politics. The ancient Greeks said, If you don't get involved in politics, politics will get involved in you. My father never was concerned about politics until someone came up to him and said you have to go die in Korea. My dad said, What is a Korea?

34 VERSE: For the Son of Man is as a man taking a far journey, who left his house, and gave authority to his servants, and to every man his work, and commanded the porter to watch.

34 REMARK: WATCH. Vigilance. Christians should be engaged, not mind numbed sports a fans and celebrity gossip experts.

35 VERSE: Watch ye therefore: for ye know not when the master of the house cometh, at even, or at midnight, or at the cockcrowing, or in the morning:

35 REMARK: You don't know when Jesus is coming, take heed to your soul. So likewise in preparedness planning. You should have provisions for any time, any place. You should take your family for field trips rain or shine then you will know if you have the right gear. In my mother's country they have snow 365 days a year. They know that there is no such thing as bad weather, just bad clothes. The master came back at

midnight. Sheeple live in a dream world, never never land. We should be eternal preppers. You never know what night will be your night. God said, Thou fool, this night your soul is required of thee.

36 VERSE: Lest coming suddenly he find you sleeping.

36 REMARK: One of my preparedness partners told me Rawlings said, He that travels alone, travels fastest. He that travels as a team travels farthest. Because you have to sleep you will find your self helpless. I was taught that J Paul Morgan surrounded his house with geese, not ducks, because they alert on anything. Geese are a great guard pet, but human partners will serve you better for survival purposes. Try to develop a network of like minded preppers, because you have to sleep some time. You don't want to wake up "dead" with your gear gone.

37 VERSE: And what I say unto you I say unto all, Watch.

37 REMARK: Jesus repeatedly says, watch, watch, watch. Vigilance, this is the essence of "prepper-dom". Watch, be vigilant, see danger afar off. Anticipate trouble. Mentally, verbally and with a group work through scenarios. Bruce Lee used to envision people jumping out around corners and mentally work through defense plans. Police and soldiers are constantly war planning. Do worst case scenario planning. Plan for the worst, hope for the best. Watch. Most people are myopic and naive, they won't survive. Be a prepper and live, you and your loved ones. I wish you the best. Watch.

PART THREE-

GOD GUNS GEAR GRUB and GET out of town

6Gs-God

You are not ready to live until you are ready to die. People need to make their peace with God BEFORE they go into battle. People who have no eternal hope engage in cognitive dissonance, benign denial and normalcy bias. They just hope against hope that everything will be OK. Hope based on nothing. People who accept that there is a probability of death can properly view the world

Under the sun, what is your probability of dying? 100%

Ultimately the hope for your country is:

If my people, which are called by my name, shall humble themselves, and pray, and seek my face, and turn from their wicked ways; then will I hear from heaven, and will forgive their sin, and will heal their land.

www.planet.infowars.com/groups/christian-infowarriors

The city of Jerusalem has been leveled to the ground eleven

times. If anyone had knowledge about how to be a prepper and survive it was the ancients.

Let's derive some wisdom from the ancient manuscripts.

So teach us to number our days, that we may apply our hearts unto wisdom. God-Prepare to meet thy God.

God-Recommended-QUOTE-Adversity breeds men, prosperity breeds monsters-Victor Hugo

Difficulties and hardships make us strong, it makes us better preppers. What doesn't kill us makes us strong. Endure hardness as a good soldier.

I will extol thee, O LORD; for thou hast lifted me up, and hast NOT made my foes to rejoice over me. O LORD my God, I cried unto thee, and thou hast HEALED me. O LORD, thou hast brought up my soul from the GRAVE: thou hast kept me ALIVE, that I should not go down to the PIT. Sing unto the LORD, O ye saints of his, and give thanks at the remembrance of his holiness. For his anger endureth but a moment; in his favour is life: weeping may endure for a NIGHT, but joy cometh in the morning. And in my prosperity I said, I shall never be moved.

REMARK-Don't make me poor or I will steal. Don't make me rich or I will forget You. We have grown fat and forgetful. Our prosperity is our ruin. The cycle of nations is rages, to riches, to ruin, God uses the word FAT. Some people think it is virtuous to be fat, dumb and happy. Ignorance may breed bliss, but it doesn't breed safety. Little piggies get eaten. People think they can bend reality by laughing at danger and playing peek-a-boo with an on coming train. Let me know how that works out for you? Meanwhile I'll built my house out of brick not straw. God doesn't say IF the winds come, He says WHEN the winds come, the house built on the rock stood firm.

LORD, by thy favour thou hast made my mountain to stand STRONG: thou didst hide thy face, and I was TROUBLED. I CRIED to thee, O LORD; and unto the LORD I made supplication. What profit is there in my BLOOD, when I go down to the PIT? Shall the dust praise thee? shall it declare thy truth? Hear, O LORD, and have mercy upon me: LORD, be thou my helper. Thou hast turned for me my mourning into dancing: thou hast put off my sackcloth, and girded me with gladness; To the end that my glory may sing praise to thee, and not be silent. O LORD my God, I will give thanks unto thee for ever.

Prepare to meet thy God-prepárate,para venir al encuentro de tu Dios.So mache dich bereit,deinem Gott zu begegnen.

Lord, behold, here are two swords. And he said unto them, It is enough.

God: For we wrestle not against flesh and blood, but against principalities, against powers, against the rulers of the darkness of this world, against spiritual wickedness in high places.

Torque no tenemos lucha contra sangre y carne, sino contra principados, contra potestades, contra los gobernadores de las tinieblas de este mundo, contra huestes espirituales de maldad en las regiones celestes.

Denn unser Kampf richtet sich nicht gegen Fleisch und Blut, sondern gegen die Herrschaften, gegen die Gewalten, gegen die Weltbeherrscher der Finsternis dieser Weltzeit, gegen die geistlichen [Mächte] der Bosheit in den himmlischen [Regionen].

==

God: He that walks with wise men shall be wise:but a companion of fools shall be destroyed-Der Umgang mit den Weisen macht weise,wer sich aber mit Narren einlässt, dem geht es schlecht-El que anda entre sabios será sabio,pero el que se junta con necios saldrá mal parado

God: It is good that I have been afflicted that I might learn thy statutes. You learn from the school of hard knocks. My tuition is blood and pain and tears. I have earned my gray hairs. The young bucks mock, but they are too foolish to realize why they won't get gray hair.

God: Most people have a house made of straw built on sand.
God says WHEN the wind comes the house on the sand falls and great was the fall of it. God allows many warning signs in our life to show us our weaknesses. A close call to a wise man is a warning. A close call to a fool is just a close call.

6Gs-2-gold

Zero Hedge informs us that gold consistently outperforms the Dow Jones Industrial Average.

Money answers all things under the sun. You will need money to execute your preparedness plan. Many emergencies can turn your paper money into sand in a hurry. Gold is the way to go. Not paper gold certificates, not silver. The one time a pilot would be happy to see the queens face is when he see it on a coin in his pocket after he ejects over a foreign land.

Ancient numismatic gold coins are too complicated. Just like people wouldn't know the difference between a 10 dollar clear stone and 1000 dollar clear diamond. Initially you should stick with reputable gold dealers and go with a knowledgeable friend. I recommend Midas Resources, Kitco and Chicago Coin Company on West Archer.

What is an internationally recognized currency in every country except America? Gold. What is currency in every country except America? Gold. Mark Dice couldn't give away gold coins to Amerikans but the rest of the world understands.

www.bit.ly/bankster-cartoon-video
www.youtube.com/watch?v=k6zpfE7WjHI

www.tinyurl.com/secret-of-oz-2012
www.youtube.com/watch?v=swkq2E8mswI

Gold-Watch Secret of OZ on YouTube

Gold-Watch Money Masters on YouTube

Gold-A quart of wheat for a day's wages

What percentage of money is cash?
3

How long does it take to devalue your currency?
3...seconds.

How long does the average currency survive?
27 years. All paper money is history collapses and goes to zero.

Gold-Money answers all things under the sun

Gold-Neo-feudalism-Poverty as a means of control-It's not be accident it's by design.

Gold-Recommended Web site-

www.prisonplanet.com/will-gold-make-it-9-out-of-9.html

Gold-Recommended-QUOTE-

"The end of democracy and the defeat of the American Revolution will occur when government falls into the hands of lending institutions and moneyed in-corporations." Thomas Jefferson

6Gs-3-guns

Guns are force multiplier. Don't buy into the false narrative the you are going to survive without guns. When you go out at night on a tactical apprehension or retrieval mission the armory asks you what weapons you want to carry. Answer: All that I can carry. You go loaded for bear. Sometimes you get the bear, sometimes the bear gets you. You have no idea what you are walking into.

Gun- George Mason: "To disarm the people [is] the best and most effectual way to enslave them."

Guns-A wise man is a strong man and a strong man retains riches. Free people own guns. Guns and weapons are a critical element of your preparedness plan. They are not the ONLY part of your plan.

Guns- By Phyllis Schlafly June, 2000 on www.Rense.com

Missionary Stephen Dunker, said when the Communists first took over China they seemed to be good rulers. They established law and order and cleaned up crime. Then one day the Communist announced, "You can see that we have established a good society and you have no need for your guns. Everyone must come in the night and dump all guns in the town square." The people drank the kool aid, just like they're doing today. The next day, the reign of terror began, imprisonment and executions. people were called "landlord" as a pejorative and were executed; a "landlord" was anyone who farmed his little plot of ground with two water buffalo instead of one.

Guns-Dr. Faria Jr., said that Batista had the Cubans register their firearms. After the revolution, Castro's Communists went door to door and, using those registration lists, to confiscate all firearms then freedom died. The people live in abject poverty to this day.

6Gs-4-gear

In Austria, my mother's country, they know there is no such thing as bad weather, just bad clothes. When you have to carry your own gear that puts a natural governor on what and how much you can carry. Some people believe you can't have an adequate pack with less than 50 pounds in cold weather. Others believe they can buy ultra light bear and get lower weight.

Gear-Take a walk every week, rain or shine, this will demonstrate to you what gear you need.

What-prep-Gear- A-TACS Advanced Tactical Camo www.a-tacs.com

Gear-Emergency Empty containers to fill with water in emergency situations. You can also use your bathtub when you know a potential emergency is coming.

Gear-Health Ranger Mike Adams and others recommend: generator, sleeping bags, fire extinguisher, first aid kit, multi-purpose knife, wind-up weather radio, weather-proof writing notepad, identification.

Gear-People need to make hiding places for their gear.

Gear-Preppers need to develop a challenge/response code word for family members nighttime I.D.

What-prep-Gear-Recommended-Web sites-
www.atlassurvivalshelters.com
What-prep-Gear-Recommended-Gear-Life straw
What-prep-Gear-Recommended-Gear-Night light that converts

into a flashlight from Ace Hardware

What-prep-Gear-Recommended-Gear-unique luggage markers

What-prep-Gear-Recommended-Gear-fanny packs

What-prep-Gear-Recommended-Gear-duffel bag

Gear-prep- the sword and the bow-basic weapons. Farming and wild food foraging-basic skills.

Joshua 24 12 And I sent the hornet before you, which drave them out from before you, even the two kings of the Amorites; but not with thy sword, nor with thy bow.

NOTE The basic weapons of the ancient world were the sword and the bow.

Joshua 24 13 - I have given you a land for which ye did not labour, and cities which ye built not, and ye dwell in them; of the vineyards and oliveyards which ye planted not do ye eat.

NOTE People in the ancient world dwelt in cities and planted vineyards.

What-prep-Gear-Recommended-Gear-mosquito net

What-prep-Gear-Recommended-Gear-water filter

What-prep-Gear-Recommended-Gear-ICE drive- A thumb drive containing important document In Case Of Emergency–and a paper notebook containing ID, passport, insurance info, emergency contacts, and medical information.

What-prep-Gear-Recommended-Article-Emergency preparedness checklist for perfect storm Hurricane Sandy – Here's what you need to get NOW Mike Adams Natural News Oct 28, 2012

Gear-Life straw

Gear-Does your night light convert into a flashlight?Ace Hardware,

Gear-Recommended-Atlas Survival Shelters

Rich people are buying underground shelters in record numbers. Meanwhile the elite use their media masters to mock common folks who buy shelters. A shelter twenty feet under the ground can withstand an atomic air burst.

Atlas Shelters is a highly Recommended shelter builder: unique ingress egress, ingenious reverse subterranean virgin soil escape hatch, dog decon room, three foot sub-panel storage, ten foot deep air burst protection. It can be a fraction of the close of concrete shelters and no paper trail.

Gear-

Recommended-ITEMS

mosquito net

water filter

umbrella

dust mask

plug converter

water pen UV

100 dollar bills

2 prong adapter

(access to printer)

apple juice

apple sauce

baton

Bible on PC

big black sturdy plastic bag for laundry

big clean clothes bag

blank CDs

blue jean pants

bottle opener

bottle scrapper

bottle water

bread

bug zapper

calamine candles

non-electrical can opener

car rental

cargo bin duffel bag w wheels

shoulder strap 4 listed clothes

CD blank

clothes pins

credit card

cups

detergent

digital camera standard usb

eating utensils

electronic mosquito chaser

fanny pack

finger nail clipper

fly swatter

hangers

health candy bars

hoodie

khaki slacks

key chain with long lanyard

knee short, zipper cargo's

laundry soap

loafer shoes

local chicken

flashlights

batteries

local milk

luggage address cards

milk

mosquito candles

mosquito net

neck tie

non-water bottle large mouth

nutella

orange juice

plain black t-shirts

paper towel roll

PC lap top

pens with clips

plain black tennis shoes

potatoes

power converter

power strip

==

==

6Gs-5-Grub

pull ups

quick dry swim trunks

sandals

scale

simple plastic slippers

small garbage bags in org box

spiral notebook with perforations

unique luggage identifier

usb memory stick for printing

vegetables

wall power cord

washable nylon black no word baseball hat full back

water filter-sawyer

weatherman tool

weave belt

white 100 percent cotton shirt

wide crush-able lady hat

yogurt

A fluoride gravity feed water filter is especially important for an urban setting. My sister was born in the city where they executed those who fed fluoride to prisoners to sedate them. Just tell them it's good for their teeth. Read the note on the toothpaste tube: “if you swallow this call the poison center.”

Grub-Recommended-web sites- www.NaturalNews.com
Grub-Recommended-web sites- www.NVIC.org
Grub-Recommended-BOOK-Seeds of Deception.
Grub-Recommended-YouTube Genetic Roulette by Jeffrey Smith
Grub-Recommended-article-Germany Prepares for Mass Flu Vaccinations
Grub-Dr Joel Wallach is a great man. You should have him tell you why animals prefer muddy water.

6Gs-6-GET out of town

GET-Don't think Boy Scout survival, think democide. In preparedness don't think camping trip, think war zone. No bunker mentality is a long term solution. No defense will stand.

GET- Joel Skousen prefers to stay in the United States. Skousen's position there will be more resistors to team up with in Amerika. He does a masterful analysis based on numerous considerations to including-nuclear power plants, volcanoes, earthquakes, war, large cities, clear land (rather than flammable forested land), sea-level , inland, fertile soil, drinkable water, accessibility by road/rail/airport, a small town (nearby for supplies).

GET- Survival expert Blake Sawyer, argues the opposite of Skousen saying that the U.S. is no longer viable and people should move to the Southern Hemisphere. With the goal of United Nations, the United States can't be allowed to remain a super power. Sawyer's concerns sound similar to the horsemen: disaster, dictators, disease, war and starvation. Sawyer recommends Argentina, Ecuador or Chile

GET-Where-Recommended-Escape countries: Many people think that Chile is a good off shore location.

GET-Where-Recommended-Song-Clutch - "Escape From the

Prison Planet"

www.youtube.com/watch?v=53qeiAVjHQU

GET-Prep where? New Zealand? Earthquakes and volcanoes, provide the country's nickname, The Shaky Isles. Is that a smart move with militant China? Do you really want to be near China?
www.prisonplanet.com/chinese-military-on-high-alert-after-it-scrambles-fighter-jets-to-counter-japanese-jets.html

GET-Prep where? Alaska? Alaska has thousands of earth quakes per year and mountain man conditions.

GET-Prep where? The best author on relocation is Joel Skousen.

GET-Prep where? Visit this web site: www.tinyurl.com/prepper-relocate

GET-Prep where? Visit this web site: www.rt.com/usa/news/leaving-us-america-country-289

GET-Prep where? Visit this web site: www.prisonplanet.com/strategic-relocation-the-film-full-version-hq.html

RESPONSE-FEED BACK

www.CaptainTonyTaylor.com

CAPTAINTONYTAYLOR

If you are concerned about health click here:

www.tonytaylor.my90forlife.com

If you need legal assistance click here:

www.anthonyhtaylor.legalshield.com

If you are interested in a preparedness seminar call 630-209-8461

If you need help with a political campaign call 630-209-8461

If you have security concerns call 630-209-8461

www.tinyurl.com/facebooktonytaylor

www.myspace.com/captaintonytaylor

www.youtube.com/CaptainTonyTaylor

www.flickr.com/people/captaintonytaylor

www.ipetitions.com/petition/Equalparenting

www.twitter.com/cptttaylor

www.DadsCustodySupportGroup.com

www.youversion.com/users/Cptttaylor

Jesus Christ is Lord

www.tinyurl.com/this-was-your-life

www.bit.ly/personal-letter2013

Please "LIKE" us at:

www.tinyurl.com/facebook-tiger-team

Please "CONNECT" with us at:

www.tinyurl.com/linkedin-captain-tony-taylor

Do Justice and Establish Equity.

CaptainTonyTaylor@gmail.com

www.CaptainTonyTaylor.com

MY RESUME:

I have skills, ability, knowledge and experience in six fields but for brevity the following is just my Security Curriculum Vitae resume.

OBJECTIVE

Captain Tony Taylor is available for seminars, media interviews and private consulting.

EXPERIENCE

- Military Security Officer

I was a Base Commander. We supported 30,000 soldiers and 40 million dollars of operations. We maintained over 150 facilities and thousands of vehicles. We monitored the air space over half of America. We managed numerous military and civilian dignitary activities and special public events.

- State Security Officer

Tactical Officer in public civilian settings and secure facilities. Training officer for Martial arts, Fire safety, Weapons, Hazard materials, Bio hazards, Search techniques, First aid, Facility security, Bodyguard, SWAT and Hostage negotiations. Facility and personal security.

- Private Security Officer

I have worked as an armed Private Security Officer with large domestic and international private security contractors. Providing high quality customized security programs to world-class commercial properties, corporate complexes, retailers, and high profile residential properties. Design, develop and implement superior customized, comprehensive, and cost effective security programs for dynamic and complex environments. Securing cash and asset transfers with armed armored vehicles in secure under ground facilities, conventional business settings and banks.

EDUCATION

I received an academic scholarship. I graduated from a military college and a Christian college. I attended numerous specialty training courses. I am totally computer literate MAC and PC. Certified in TV/video production and editing equipment. AA

PERSONAL

I have lived in numerous locations domestically and internationally. I exercise daily. I have a high end class C drivers license. CDL I am a seven year infowarrior.

THANKS

I would like to thank Professor Slattery. Professor Slattery is a survivor. He is one of the last Korean War atomic soldiers.

He is one of the survivors of THE most battle hardened units in the military, the Rakkasans. What does "survivor" mean?

If you look up "survivor" in the dictionary this man's face should come up.

www.facebook.com/thomas.j.slattery

You know you're a survivor when:

...you show up at the class reunion and you're the last one left.

...when you get promoted because all the officers got killed off.

...your unit has 5000 going in and 2000 coming out.

...when you past octogenarian years ago and can still quote limericks until midnight.

...when your rifle got stripped off on your first combat jump and you live to tell about it.

...when your family came to America with a knot of the back of their head and their last recollection was sitting in a pub.

www.ingramcontent.com/pod-product-compliance
Ingram Content Group UK Ltd.
Pitfield, Milton Keynes, MK11 3LW, UK
UKHW020241250726
13967UKWH00001B/498